Novel

8-10 yrs.

THE SMOKE FROM GASOLINE ALLEY

A Cartoon Story for New Children

THE SMOKE FROM GASOLINE ALLEY

A Cartoon Story for New Children

A Gasoline Alley Book

by

Dick Moores

With an Afterword for Parents and Teachers
By
Ralph Nader

Sheed and Ward, Inc.
Subsidiary of Universal Press Syndicate
Kansas City

The "Cartoon Stories for New Children Series" is edited by Garry Trudeau, creator of "Doonesbury." Future selections will include the contributions of a number of other distinguished cartoonists and illustrators whose work is well known to newspaper audiences.

Already released are:

What is God's Area Code?
A Kelly-Duke Book by Jack Moore

Joanie
A Doonesbury Book by G. B. Trudeau

"Francine, Your Face Would Stop a Clock"
A Miss Peach Book by Mell Lazarus

We'll Take it From Here, Sarge
A Doonesbury Book by G. B. Trudeau

Let's See if Anyone Salutes
A Steve Canyon Book by Milton Caniff

Copyright © 1976 by the Chicago Tribune
Afterword Copyright © 1976 by Ralph Nader

Library of Congress Cataloging in Publication Data

Moores, Dick.
   The smoke from Gasoline Alley.

   (Cartoon stories for new children)
   SUMMARY: Concerned over car pollution Nina Wallet buries her car keys and decides to walk everywhere, but her plan backfires.
   1. Automobiles — Environmental aspects — Juvenile literature. 2. Automobiles — Motors — Exhaust gas — Juvenile literature. [1. Automobiles — Environmental aspects. 2. Pollution] I. Title
TL154.M58   ·   363.6   75-45171
ISBN O-8362-0670-3

To Gretchen

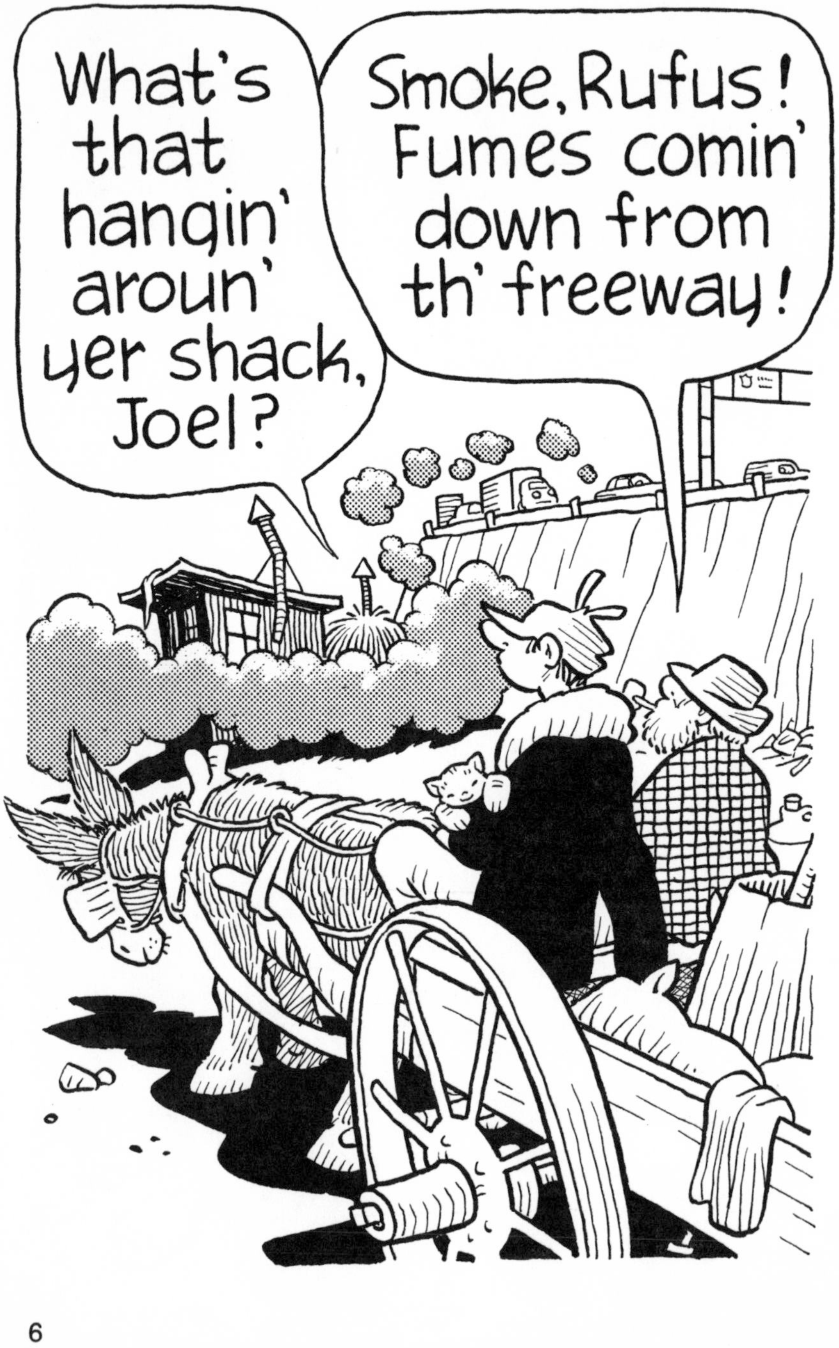
What's that hangin' aroun' yer shack, Joel?
Smoke, Rufus! Fumes comin' down from th' freeway!

Right poor when a man got t' beat his way into his own house with a shovel!

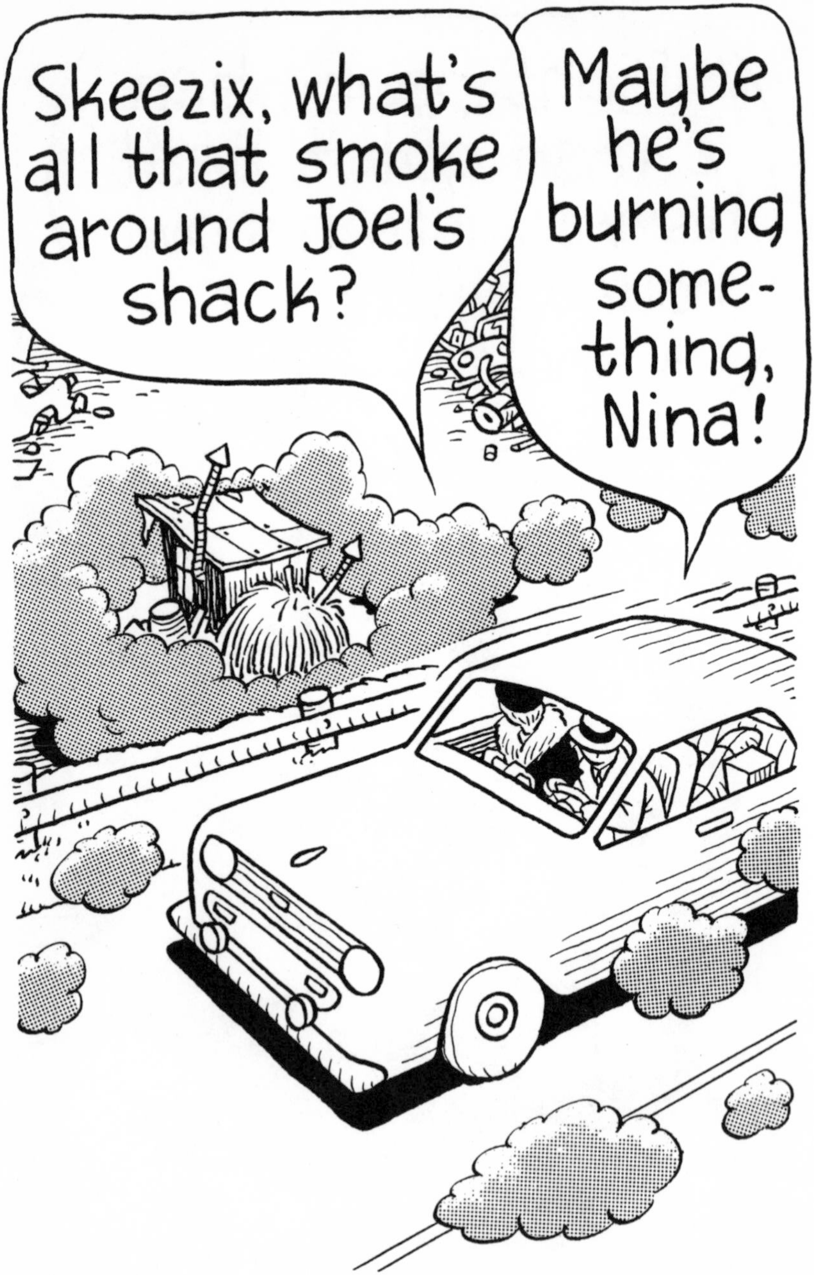
Skeezix, what's all that smoke around Joel's shack?
Maybe he's burning some-thing, Nina!

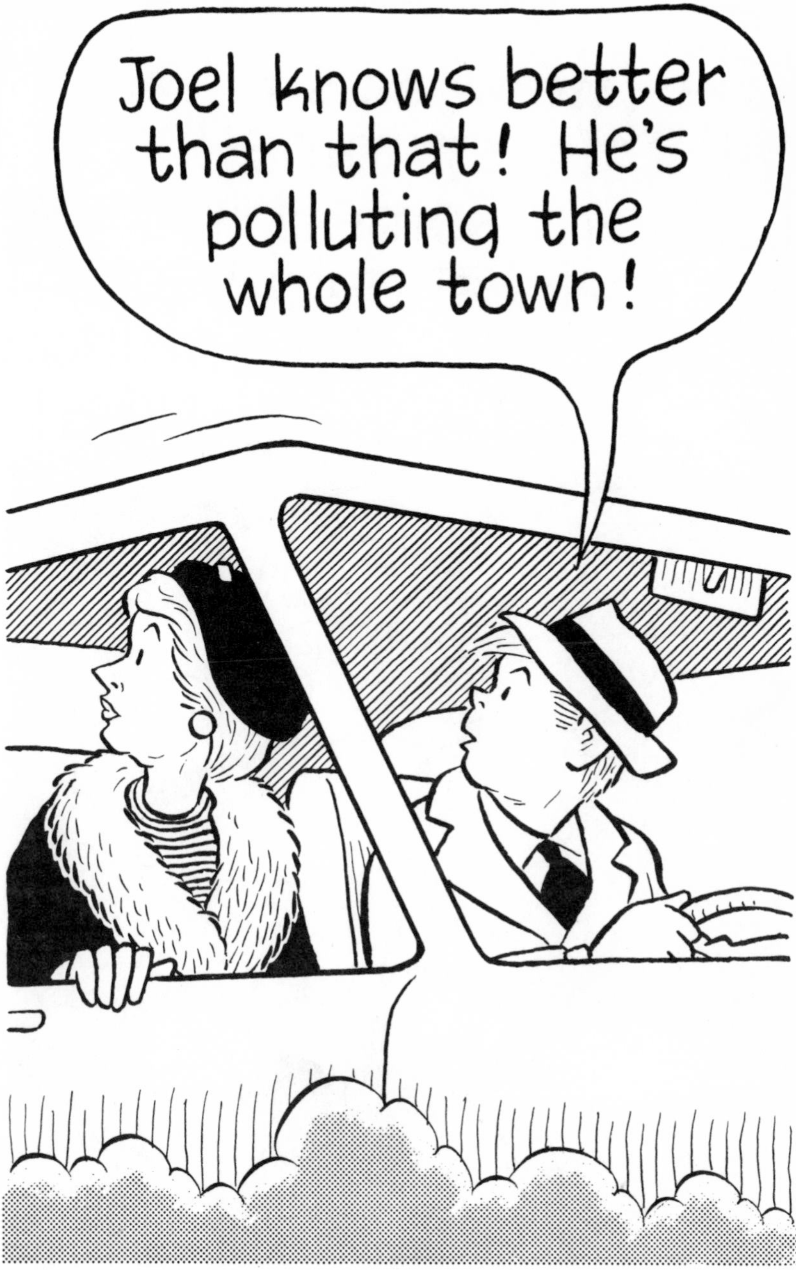
Joel knows better than that! He's polluting the whole town!

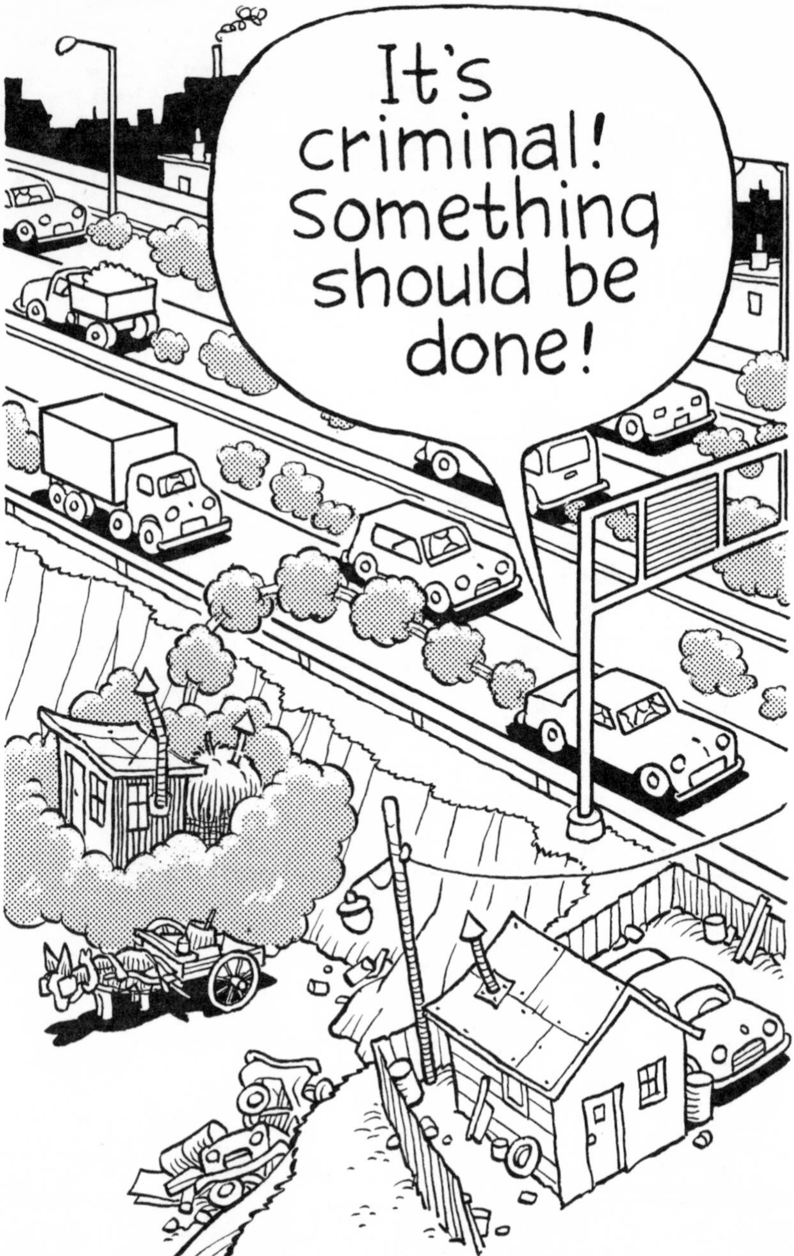
It's criminal! Something should be done!

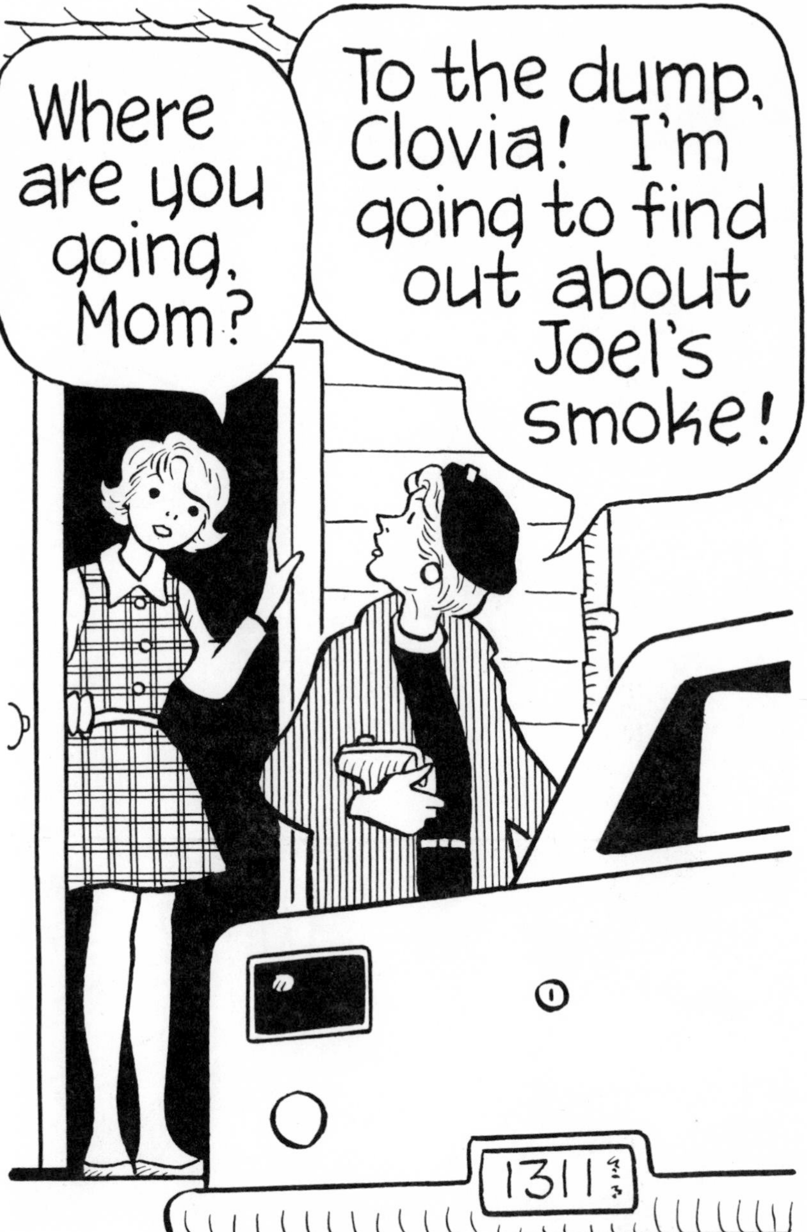
Where are you going, Mom?
To the dump, Clovia! I'm going to find out about Joel's smoke!
1311

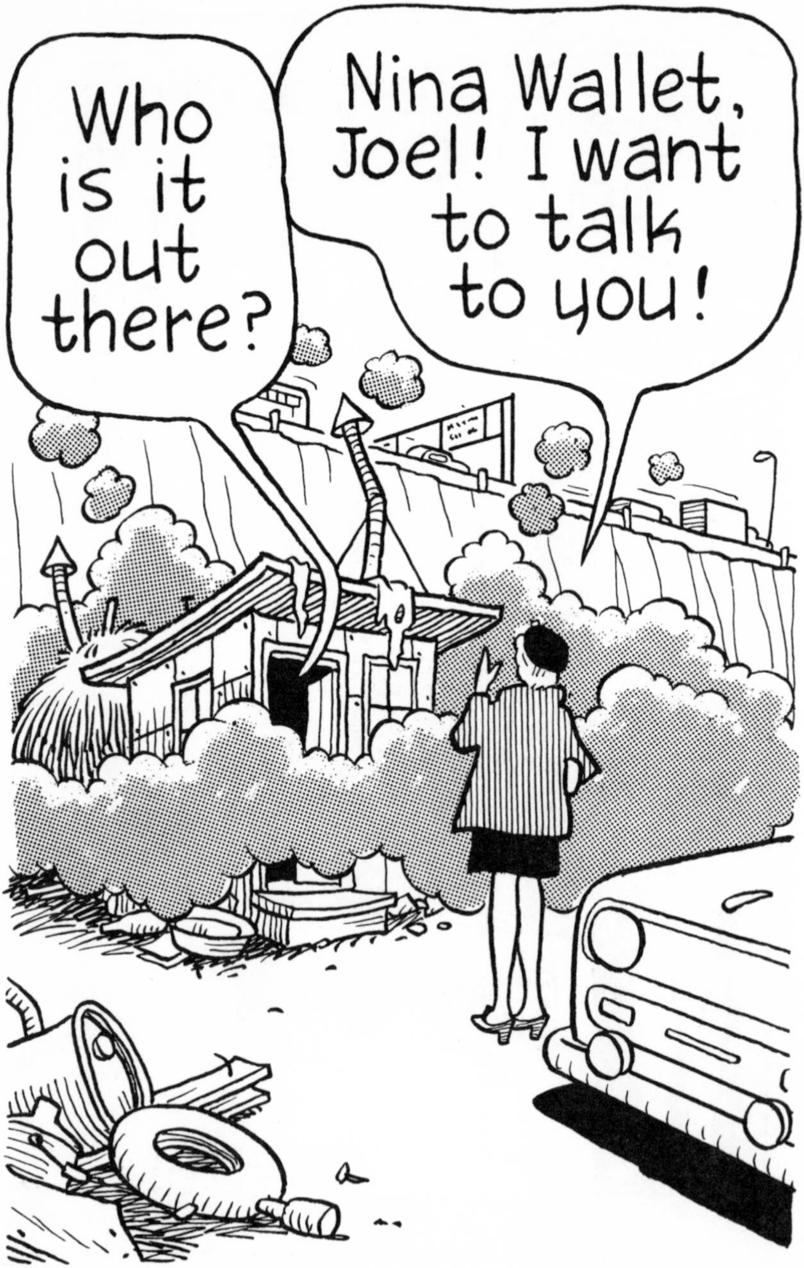
Who is it out there?
Nina Wallet, Joel! I want to talk to you!

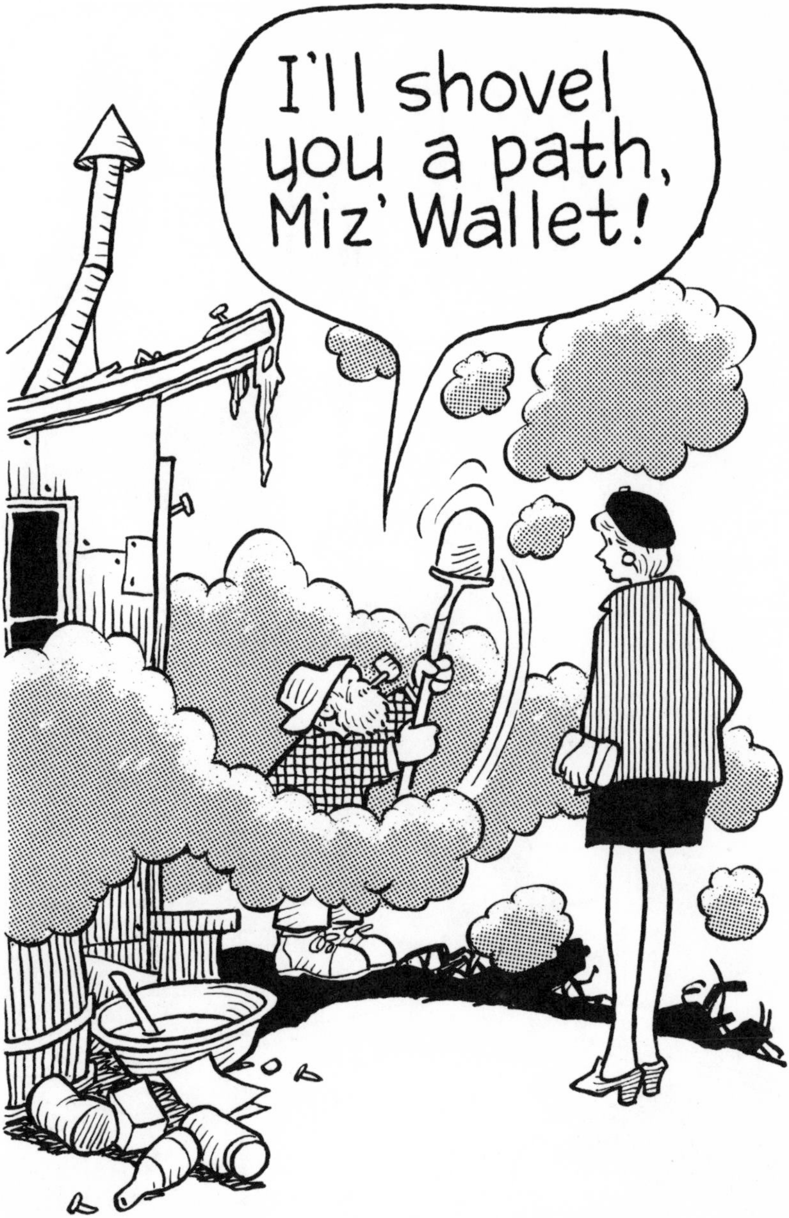
I'll shovel you a path, Miz' Wallet!

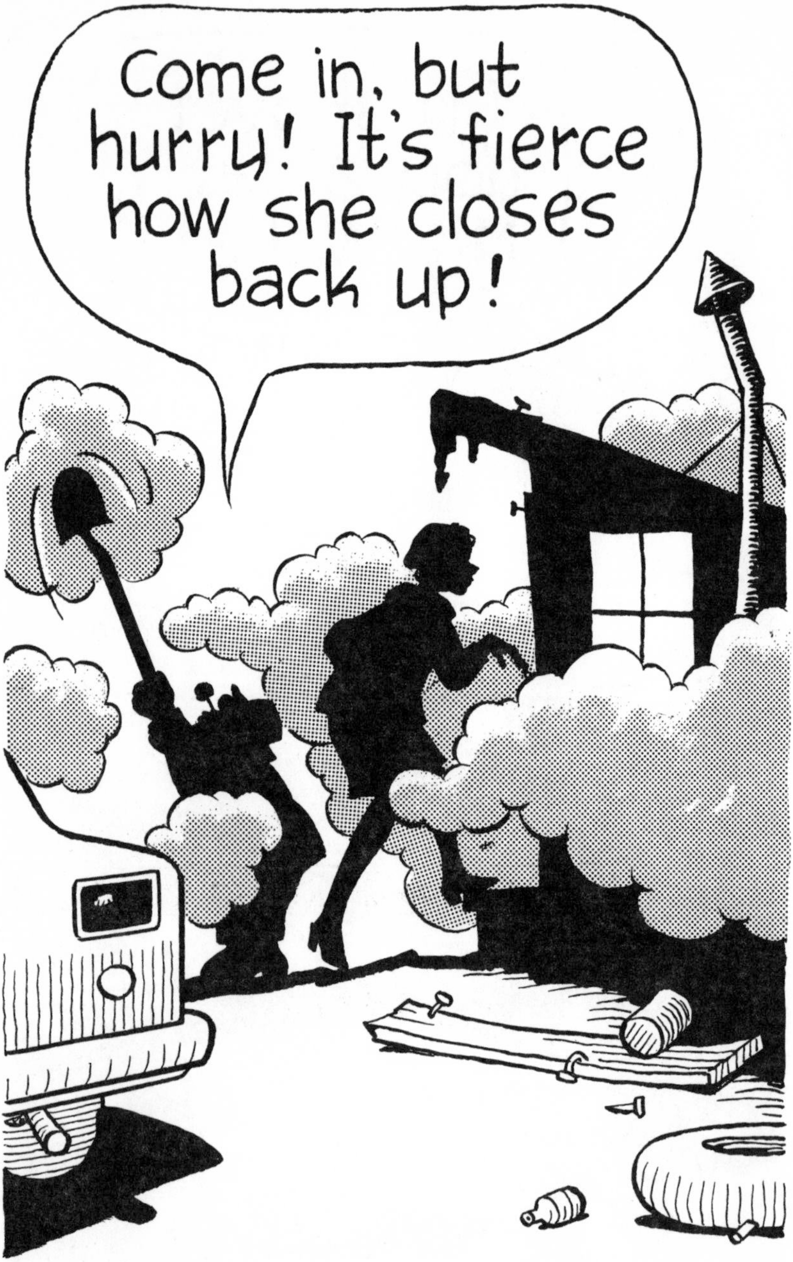
Come in, but hurry! It's fierce how she closes back up!

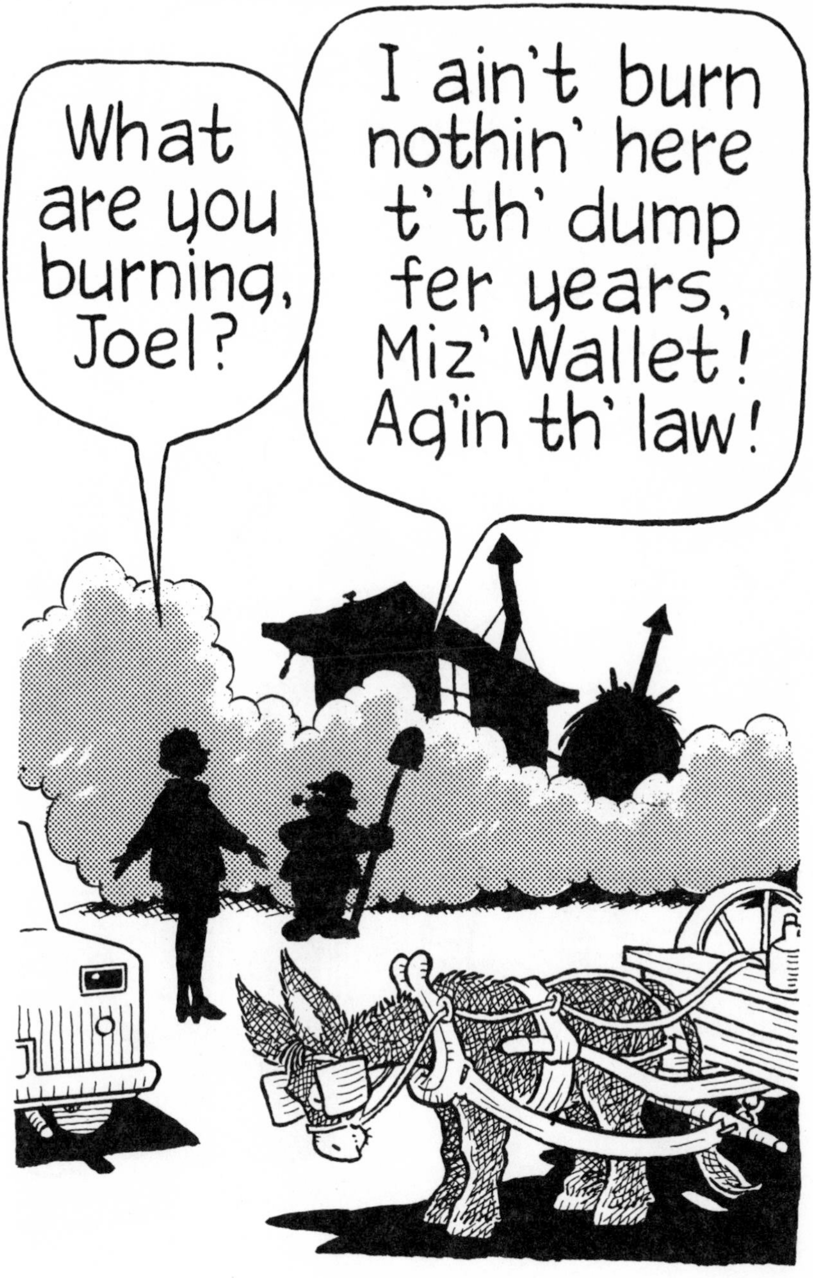
What are you burning, Joel?
I ain't burn nothin' here t' th' dump fer years, Miz' Wallet! Ag'in th' law!

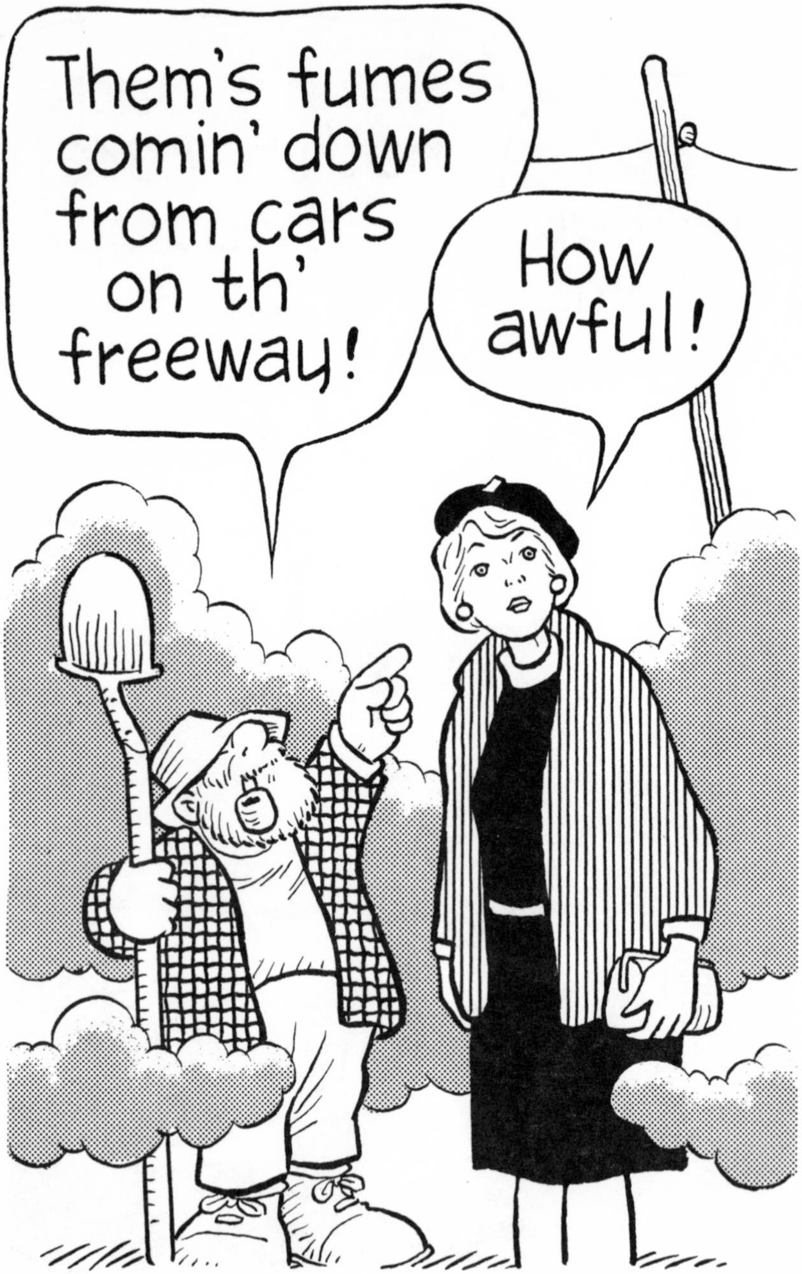
Them's fumes comin' down from cars on th' freeway!
How awful!

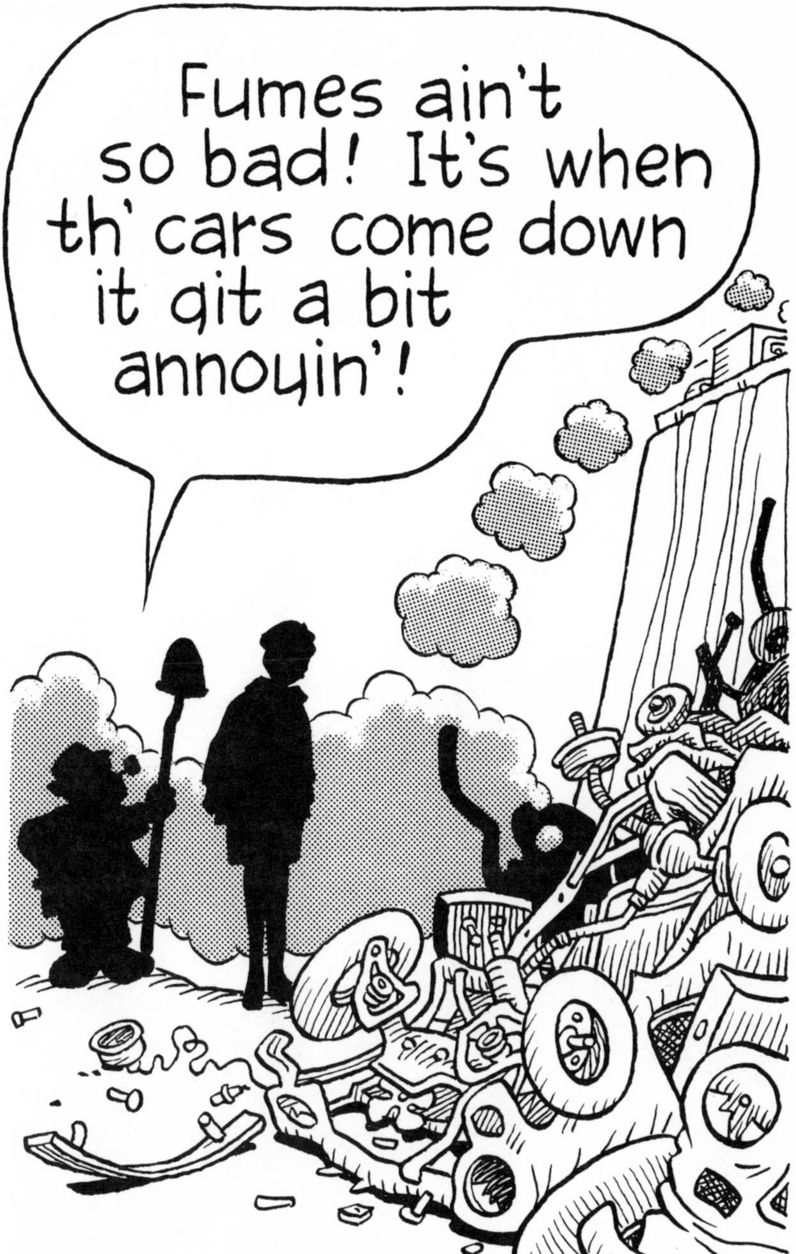
Fumes ain't so bad! It's when th' cars come down it git a bit annoyin'!

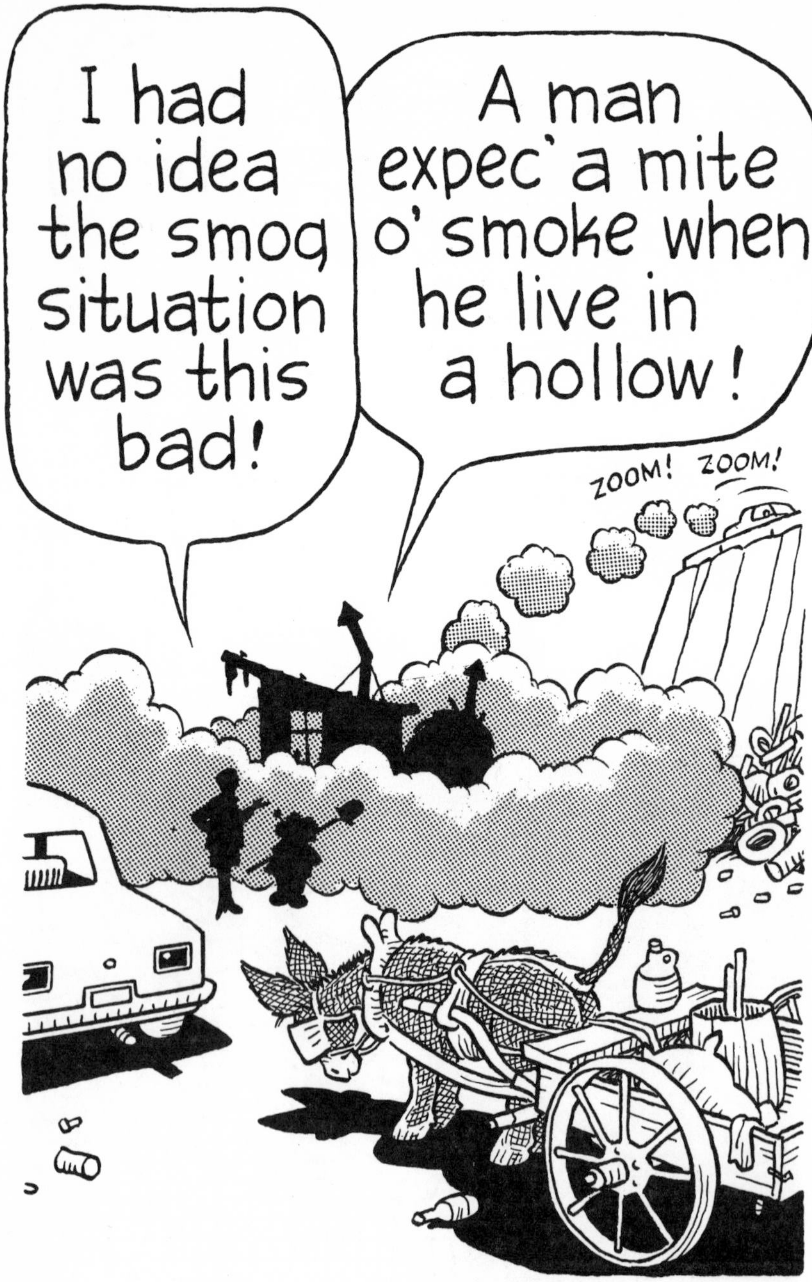
I had no idea the smog situation was this bad!
A man expec' a mite o' smoke when he live in a hollow!
ZOOM! ZOOM!

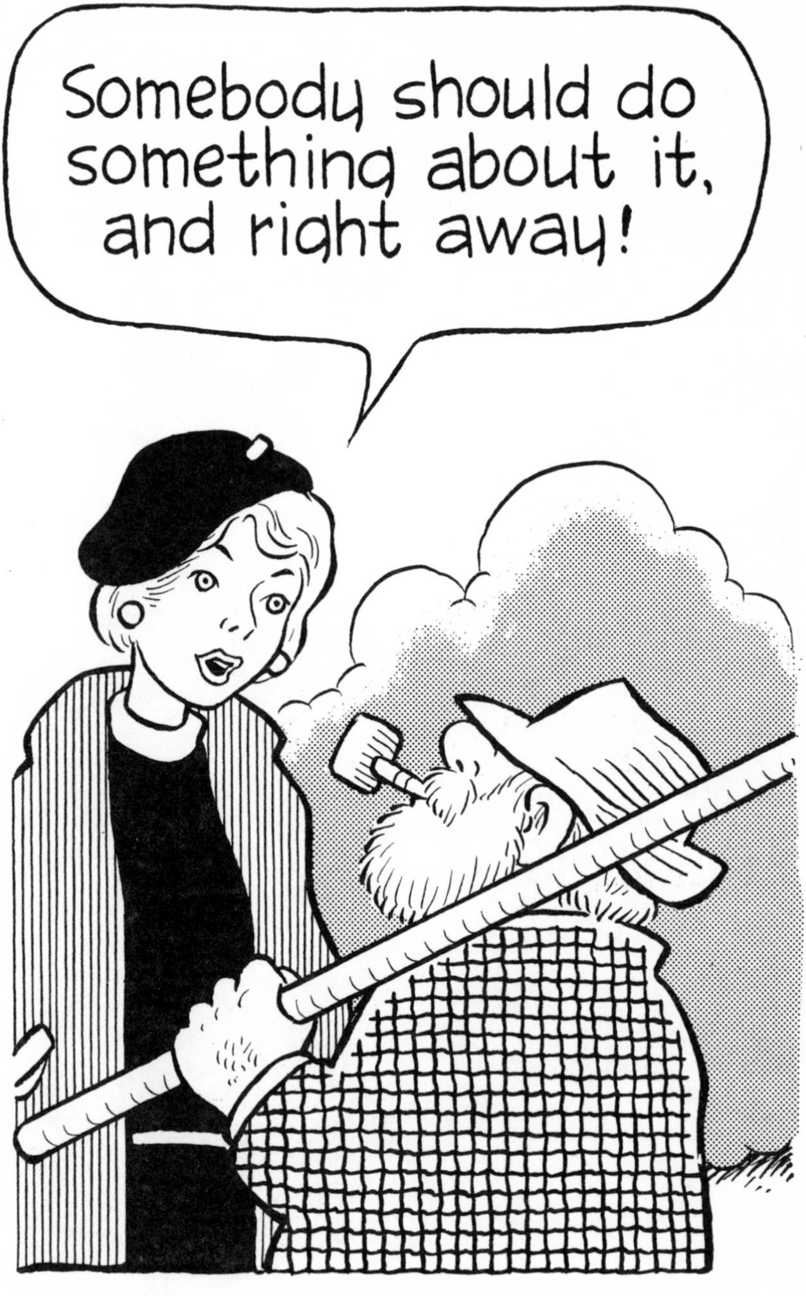
Somebody should do something about it, and right away!

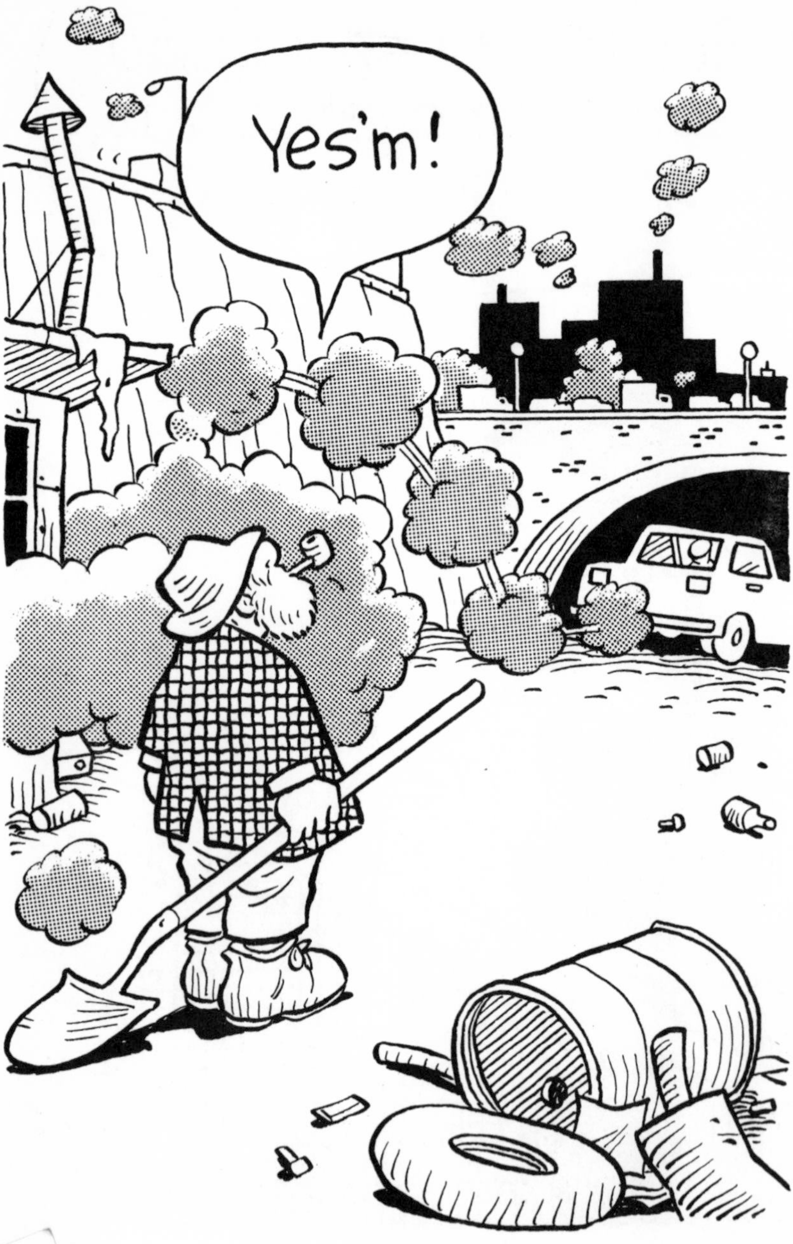
Yes'm!

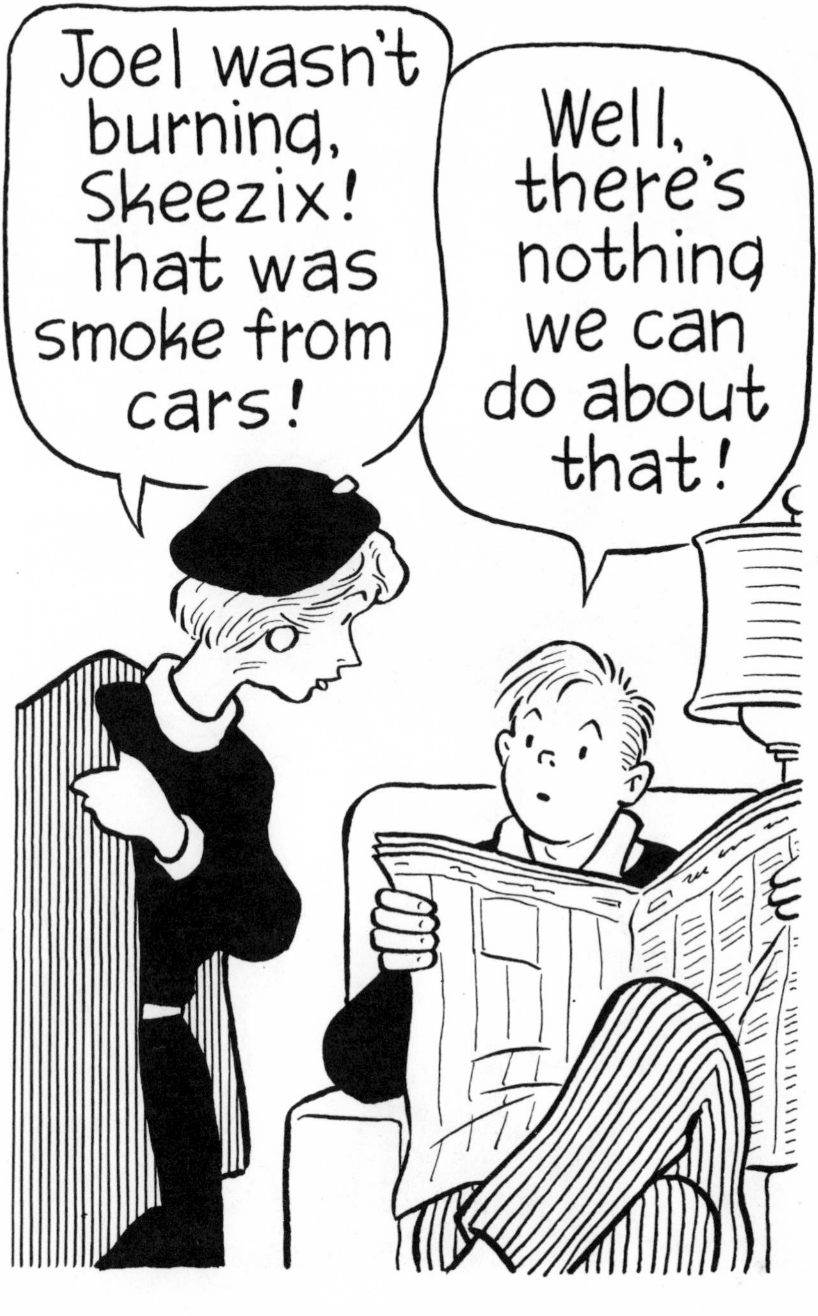
Joel wasn't burning, Skeezix! That was smoke from cars!
Well, there's nothing we can do about that!

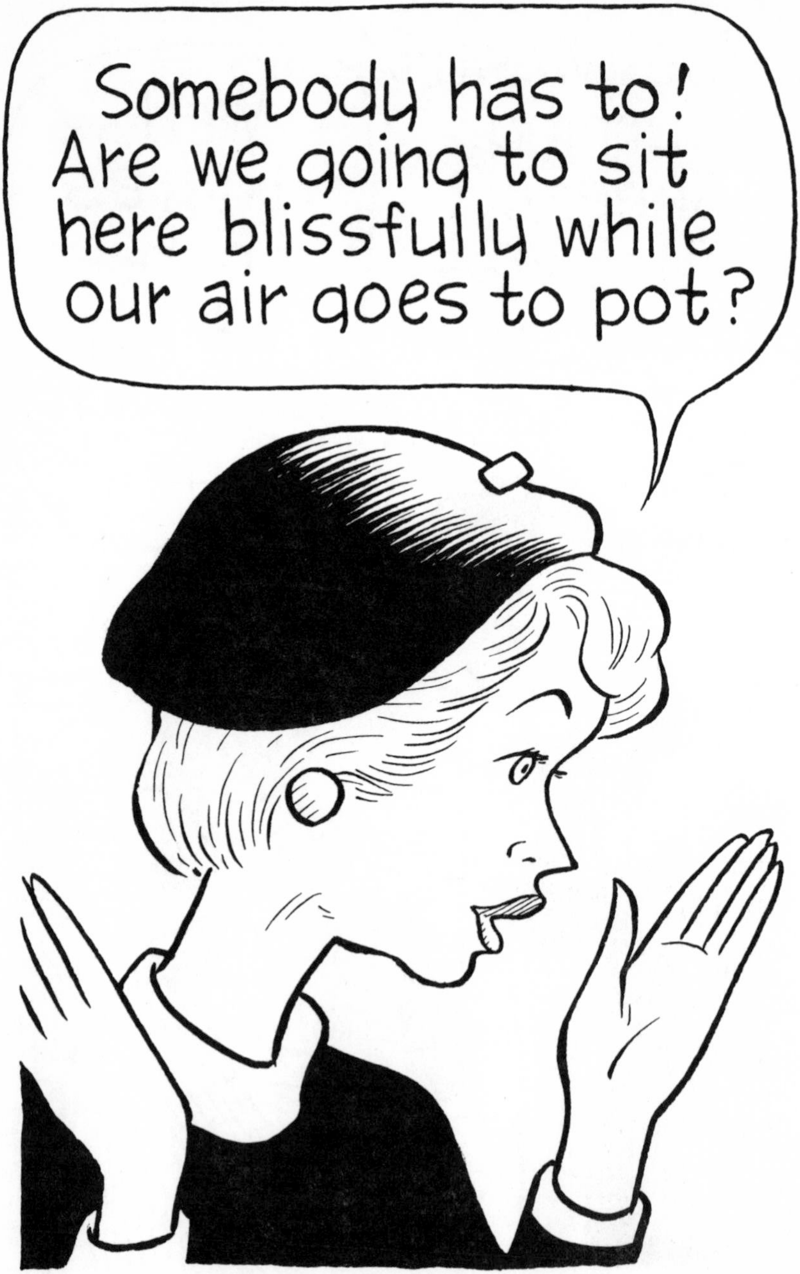
Somebody has to! Are we going to sit here blissfully while our air goes to pot?

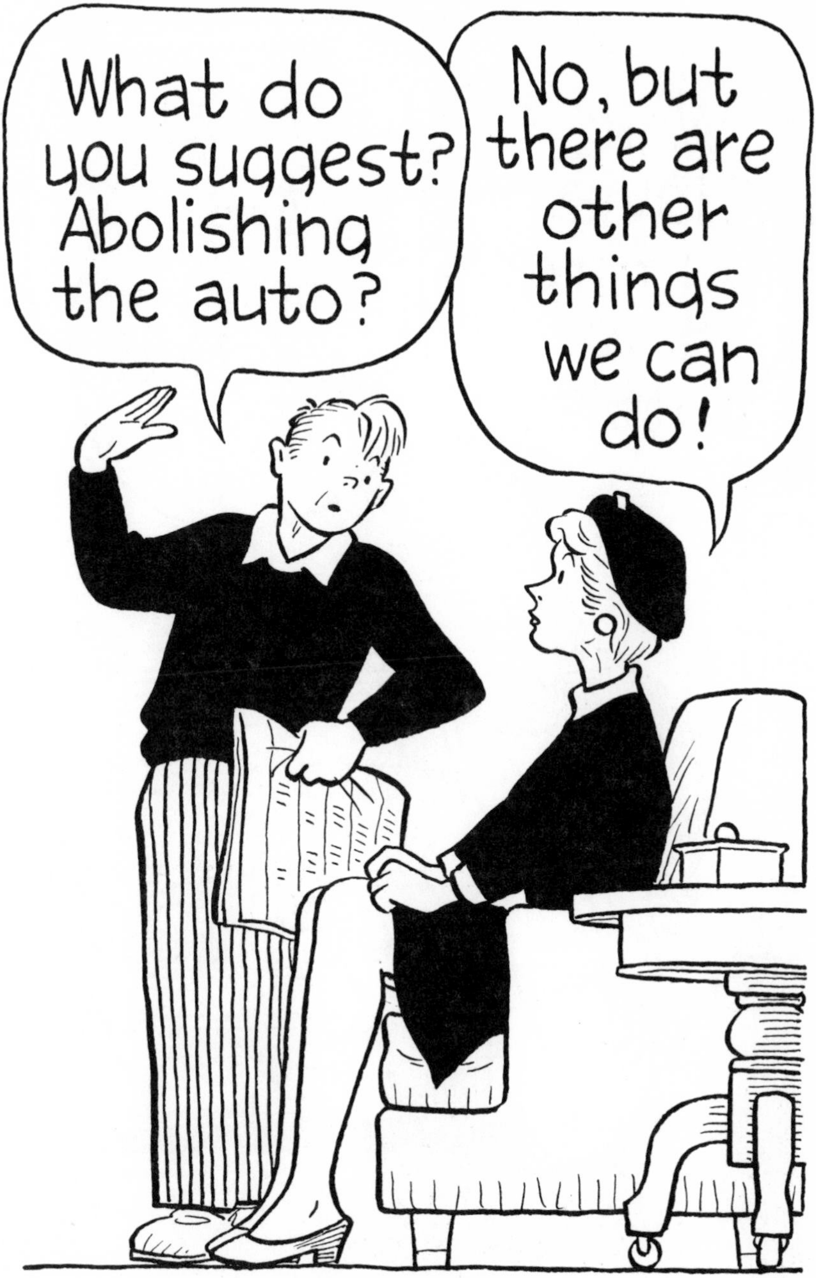
What do you suggest? Abolishing the auto?
No, but there are other things we can do!

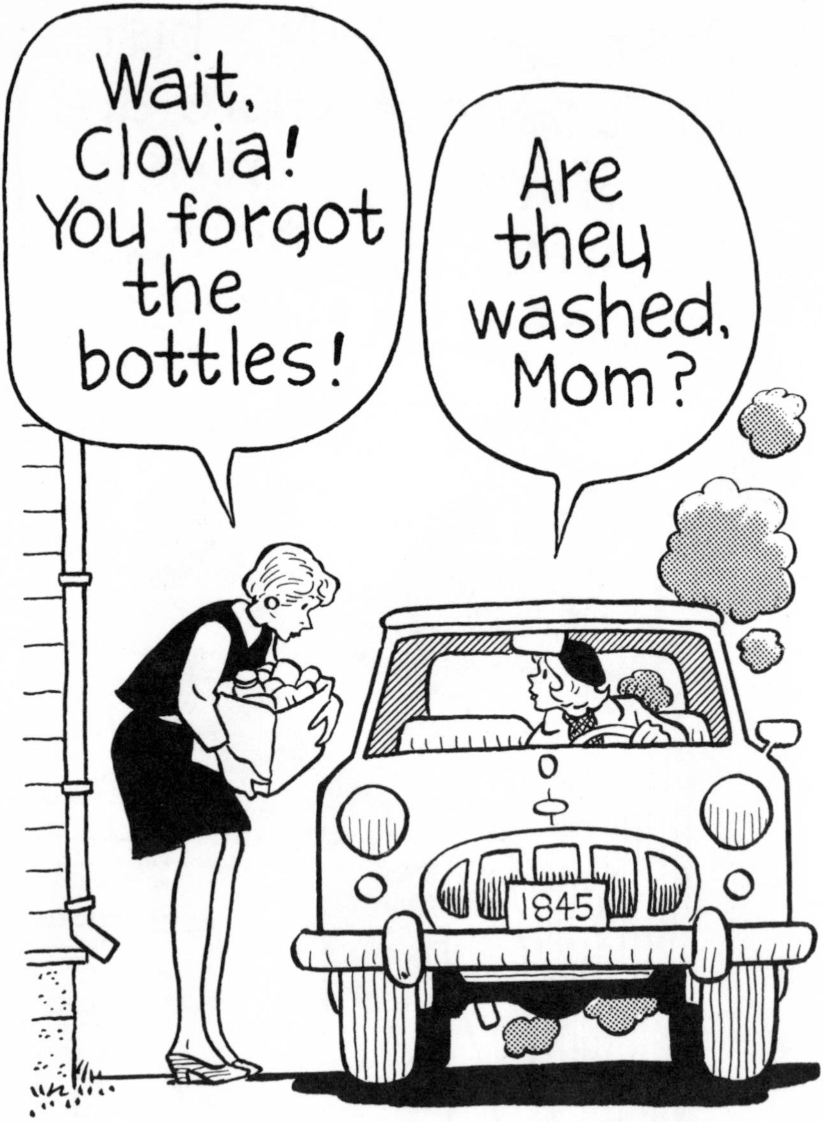
Wait, Clovia! You forgot the bottles!
Are they washed, Mom?
1845

Yes, ready for recycling! There's a station on the parking lot at the bank!
I know!

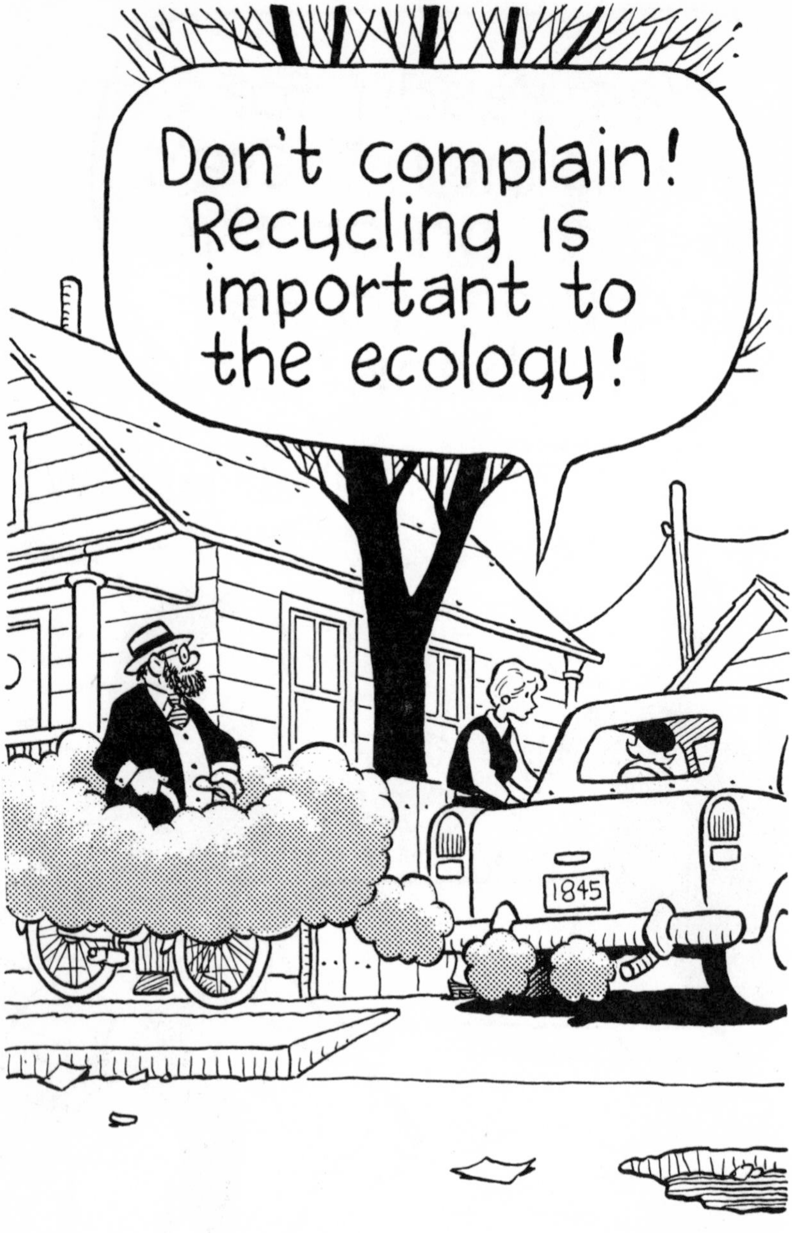
Don't complain! Recycling is important to the ecology!
1845

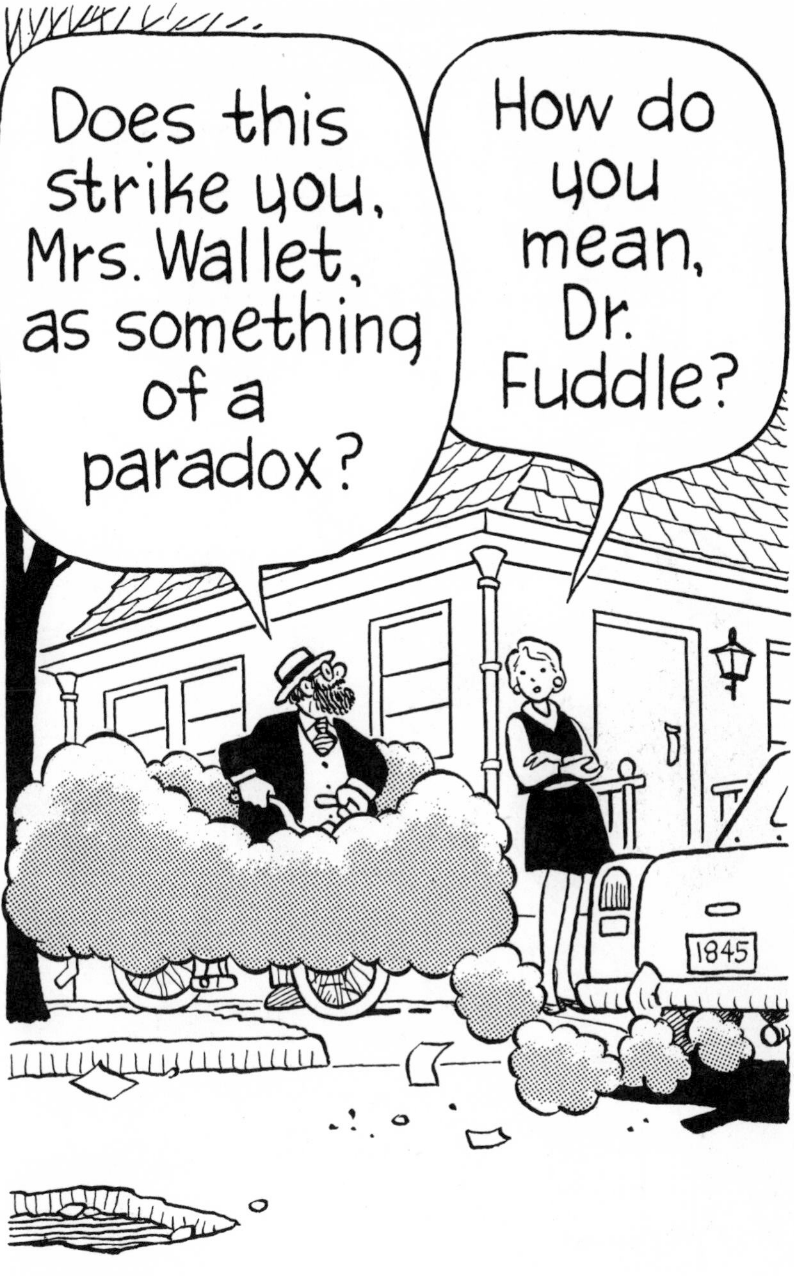
Does this strike you, Mrs. Wallet, as something of a paradox?
How do you mean, Dr. Fuddle?
1845

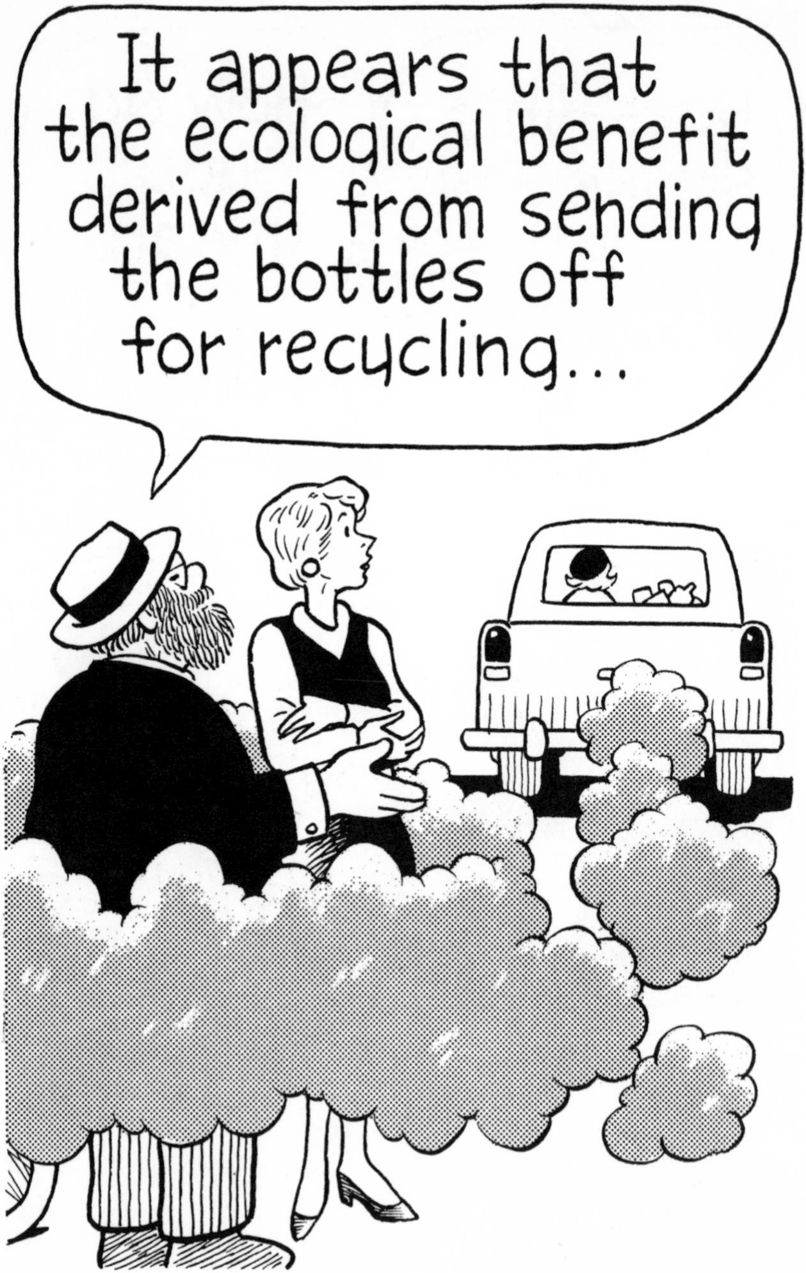
It appears that the ecological benefit derived from sending the bottles off for recycling...

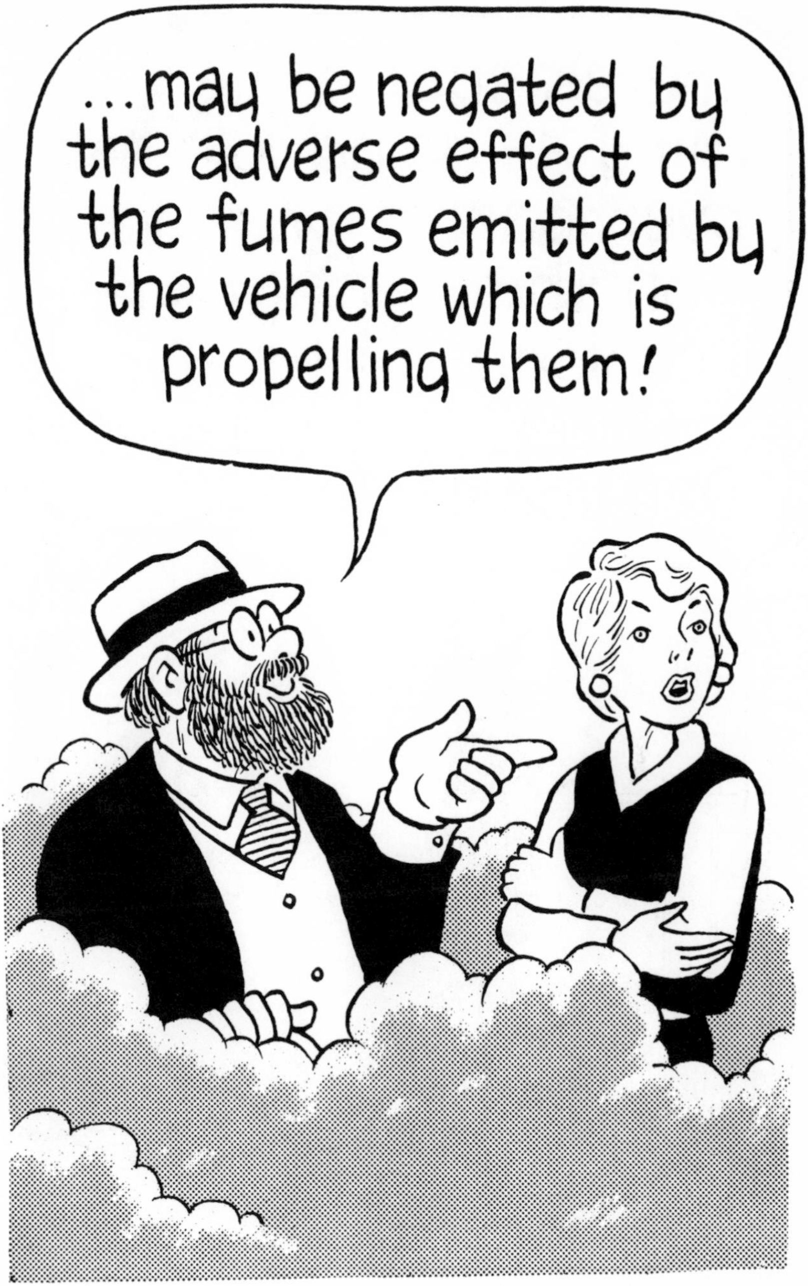
...may be negated by the adverse effect of the fumes emitted by the vehicle which is propelling them!

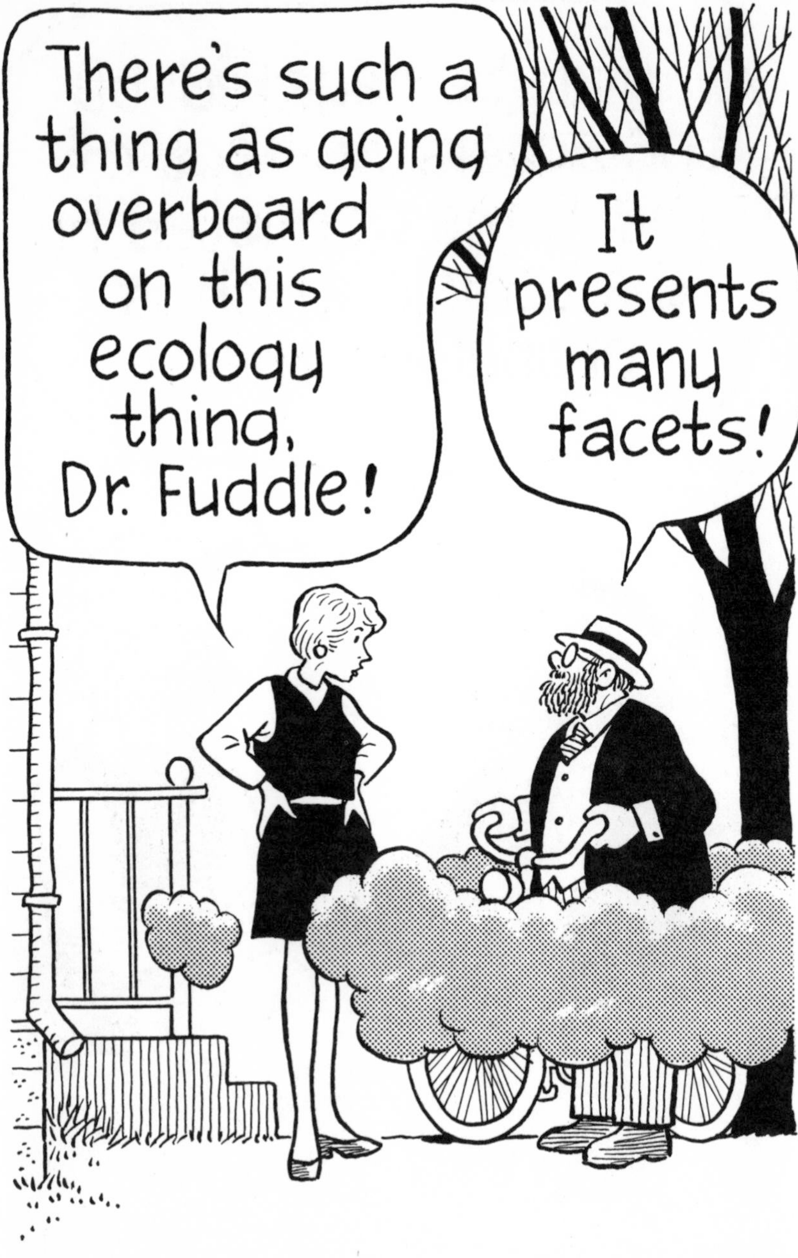
There's such a thing as going overboard on this ecology thing, Dr. Fuddle!
It presents many facets!

I use biodegradable products! I don't burn! I have a compost pit!

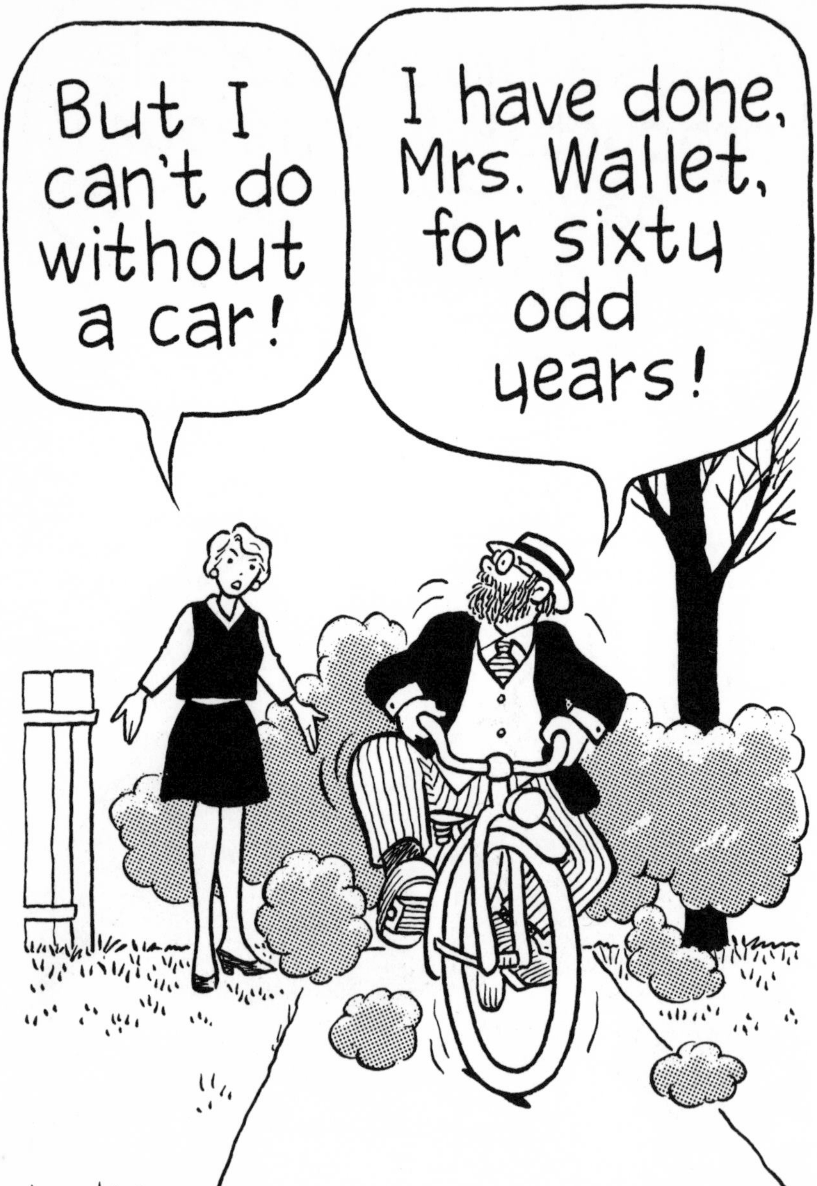
But I can't do without a car!
I have done, Mrs. Wallet, for sixty odd years!

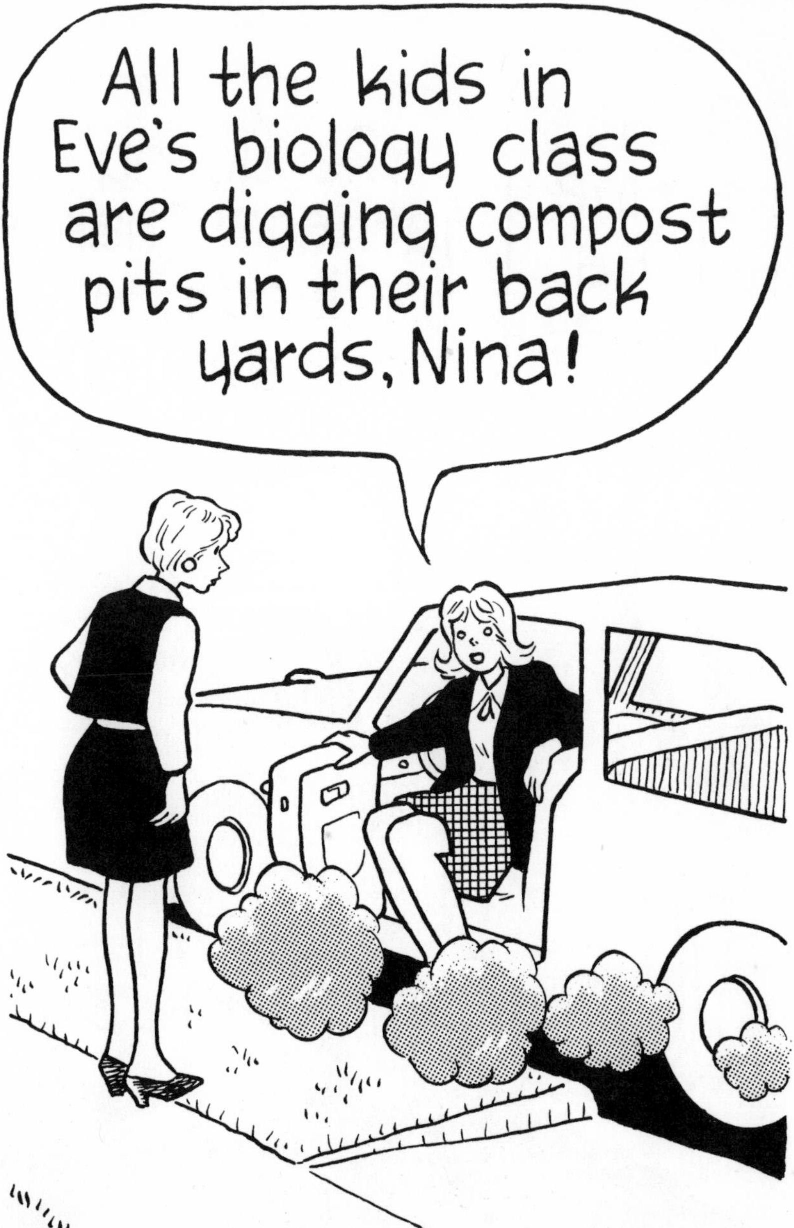
All the kids in Eve's biology class are digging compost pits in their back yards, Nina!

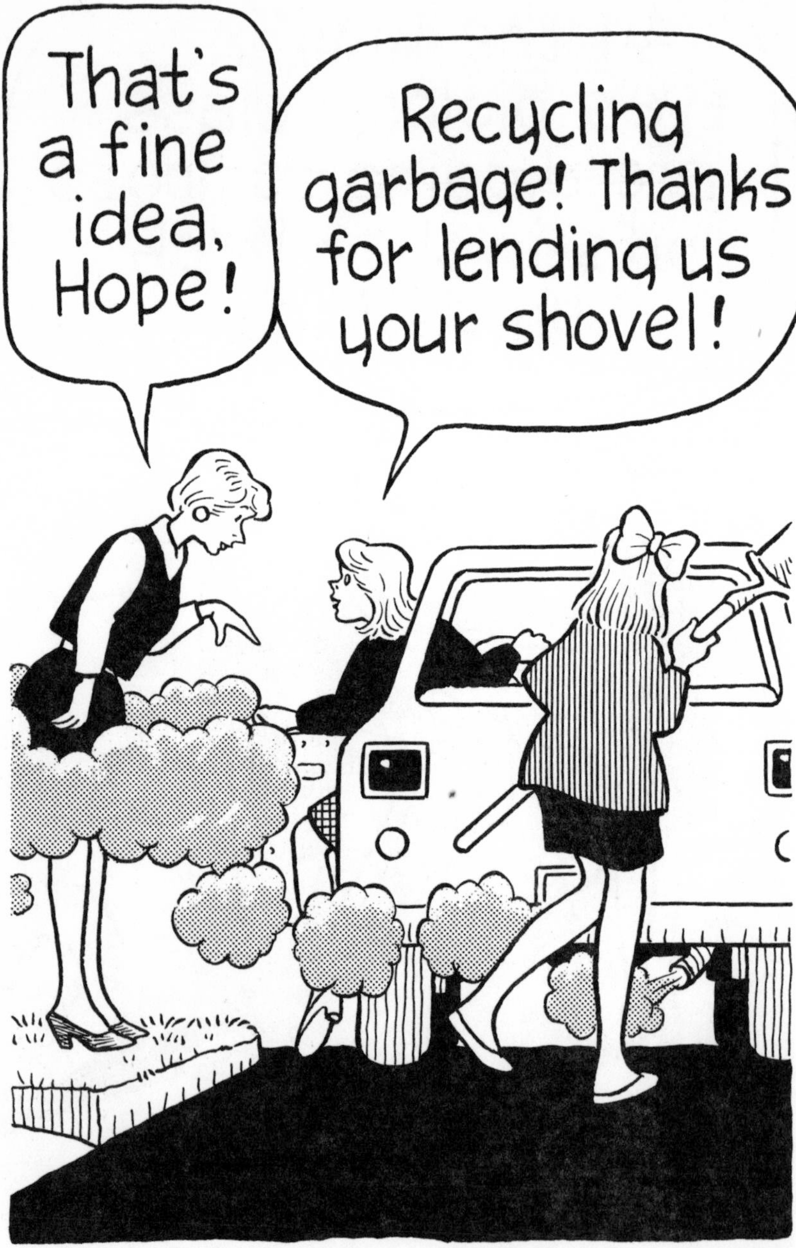
That's a fine idea, Hope!
Recycling garbage! Thanks for lending us your shovel!

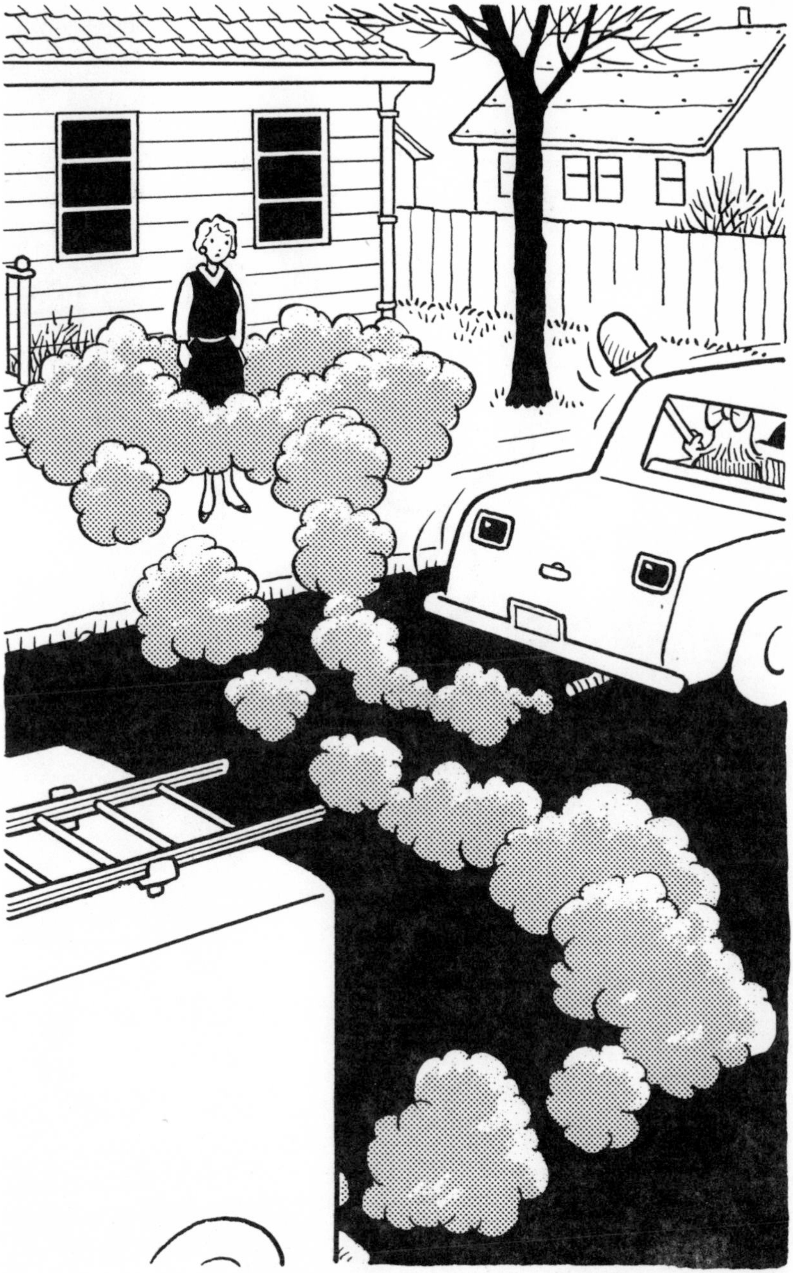

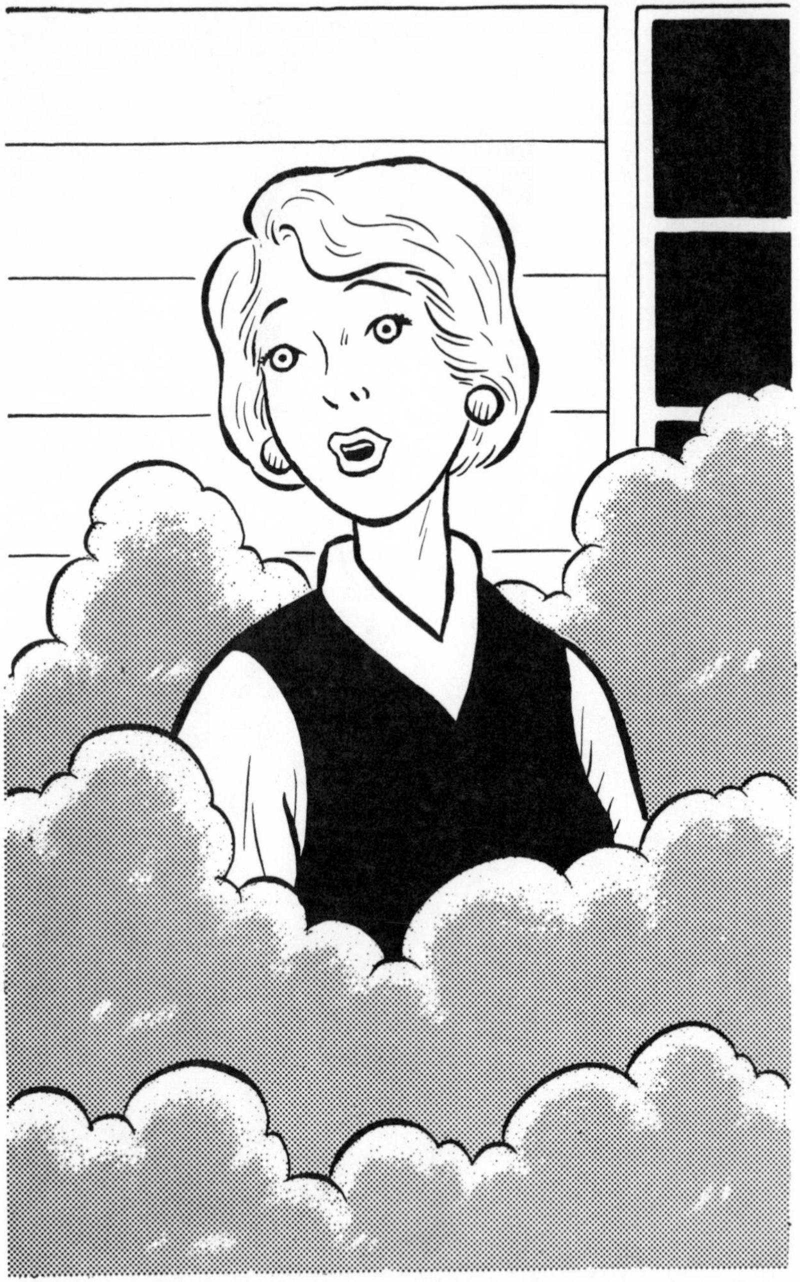

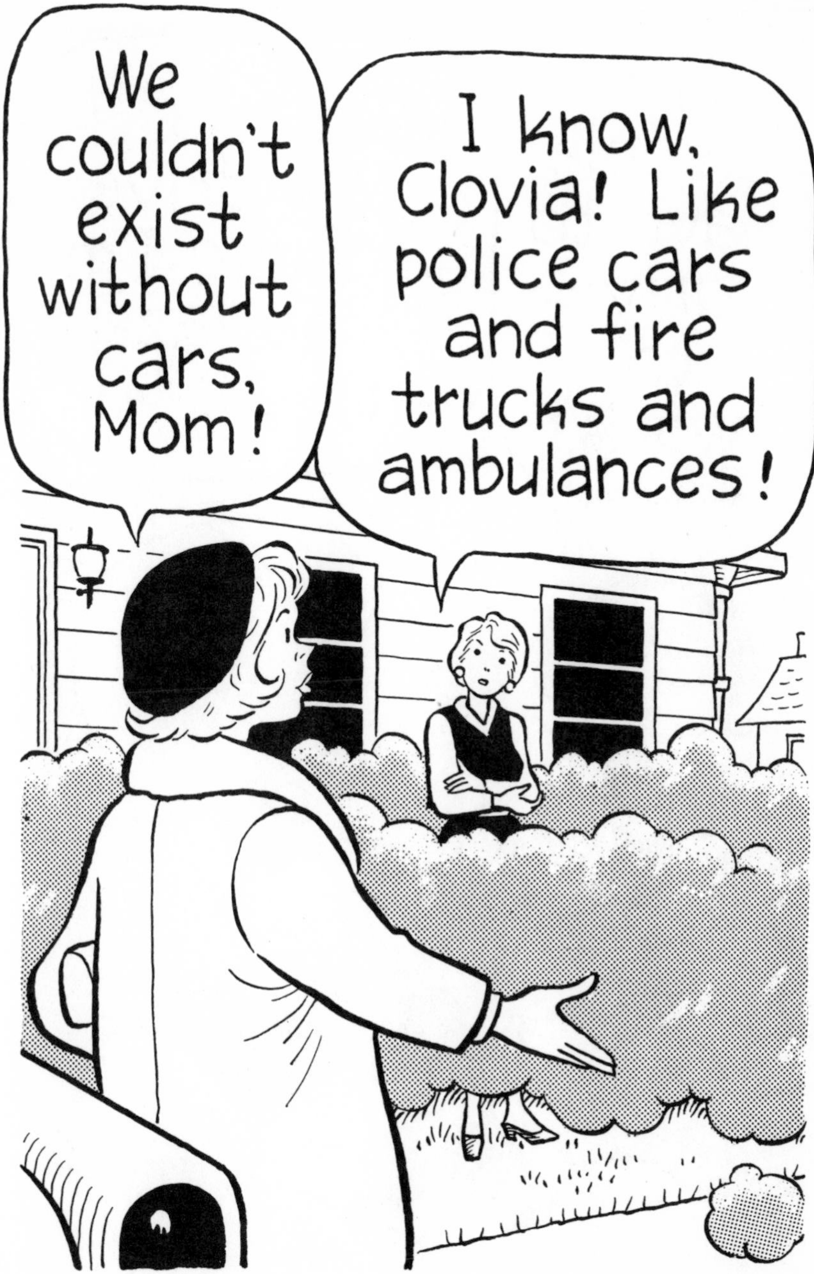
We couldn't exist without cars, Mom!
I know, Clovia! Like police cars and fire trucks and ambulances!

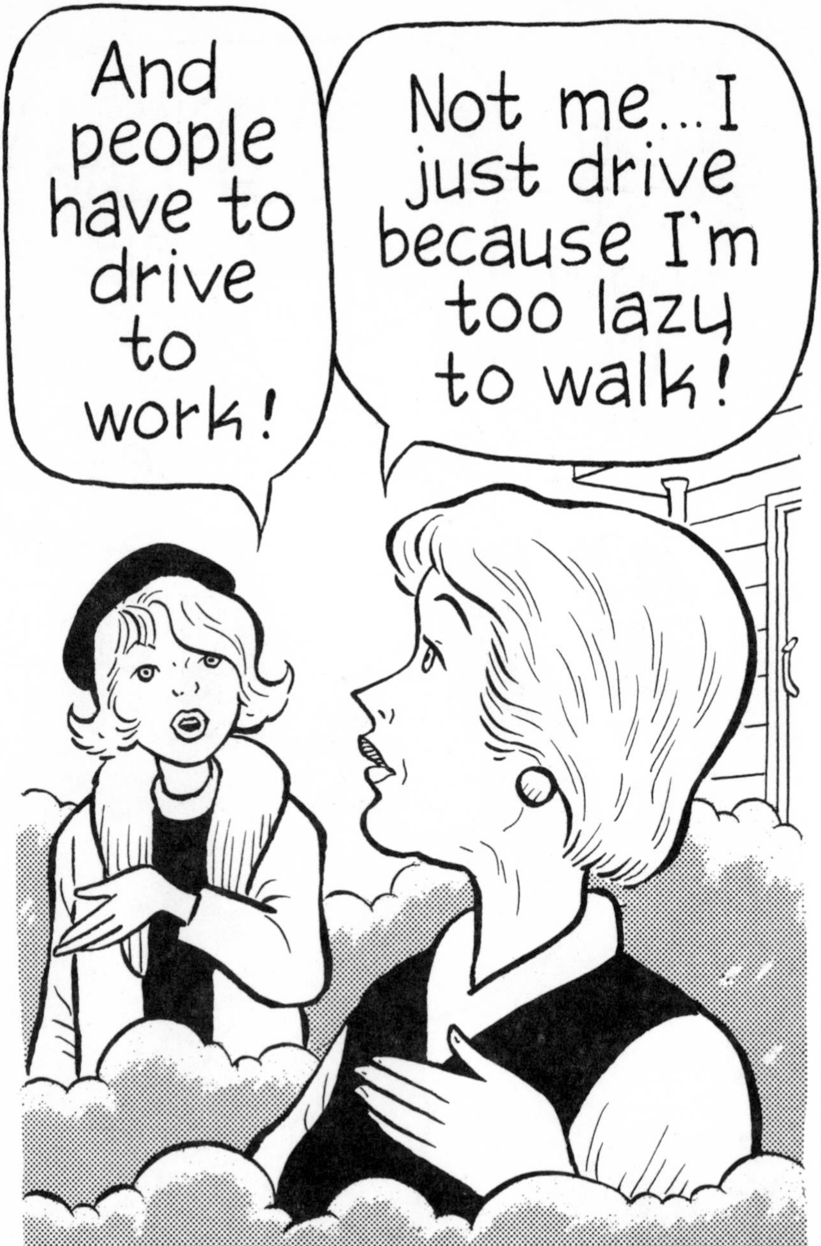
And people have to drive to work!
Not me... I just drive because I'm too lazy to walk!

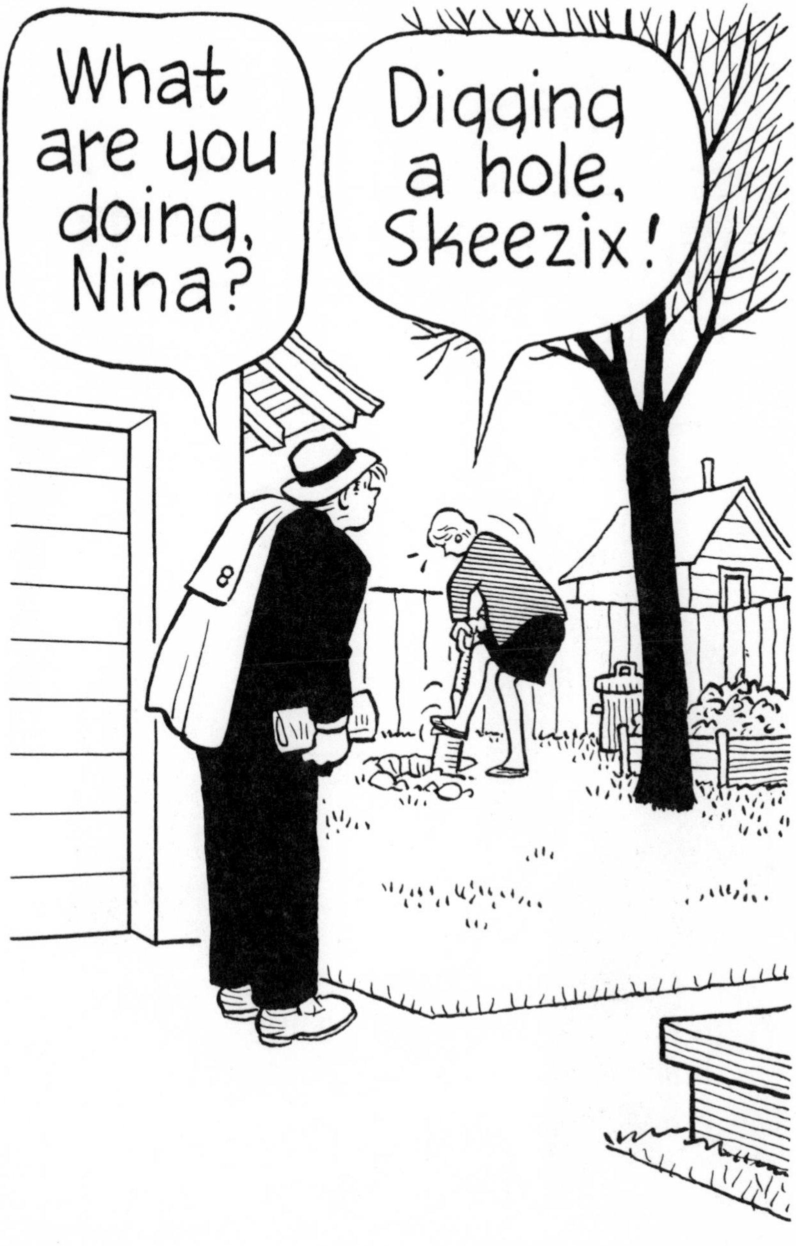
What are you doing, Nina?
Digging a hole, Skeezix!

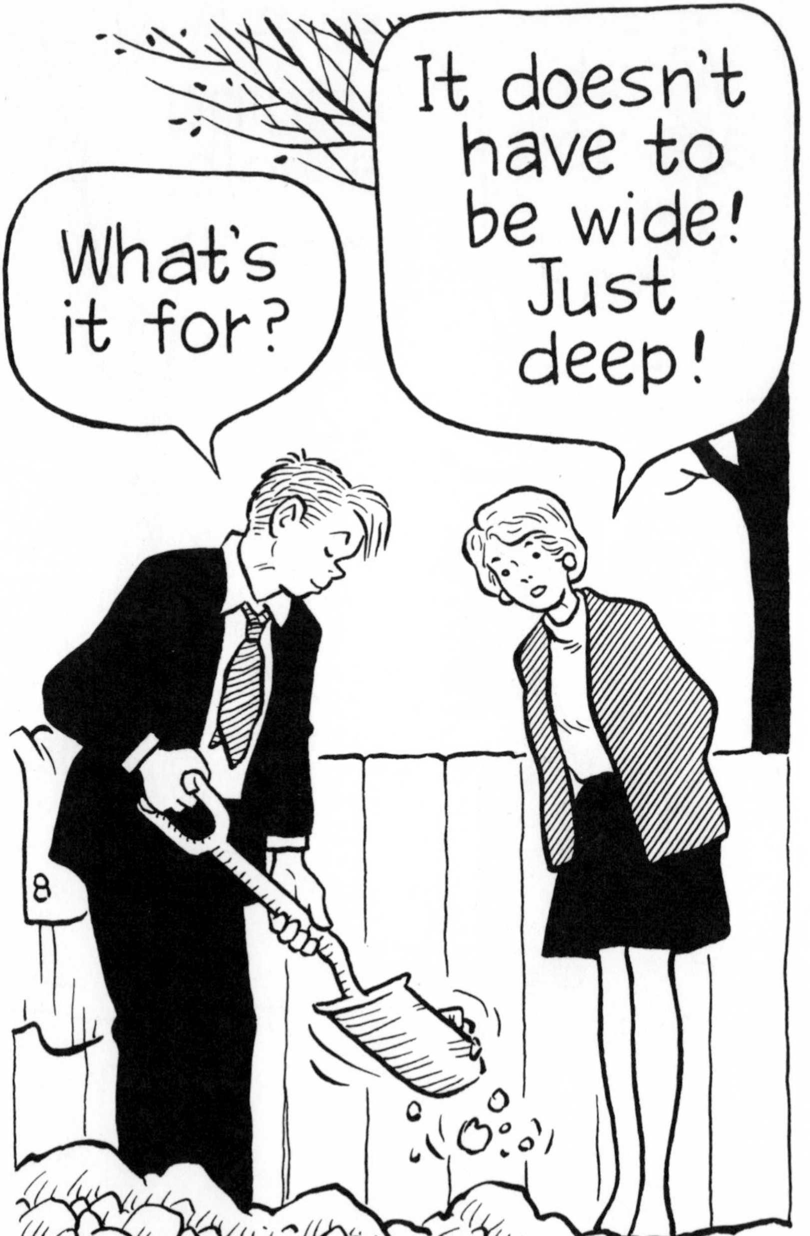
What's it for?
It doesn't have to be wide! Just deep!

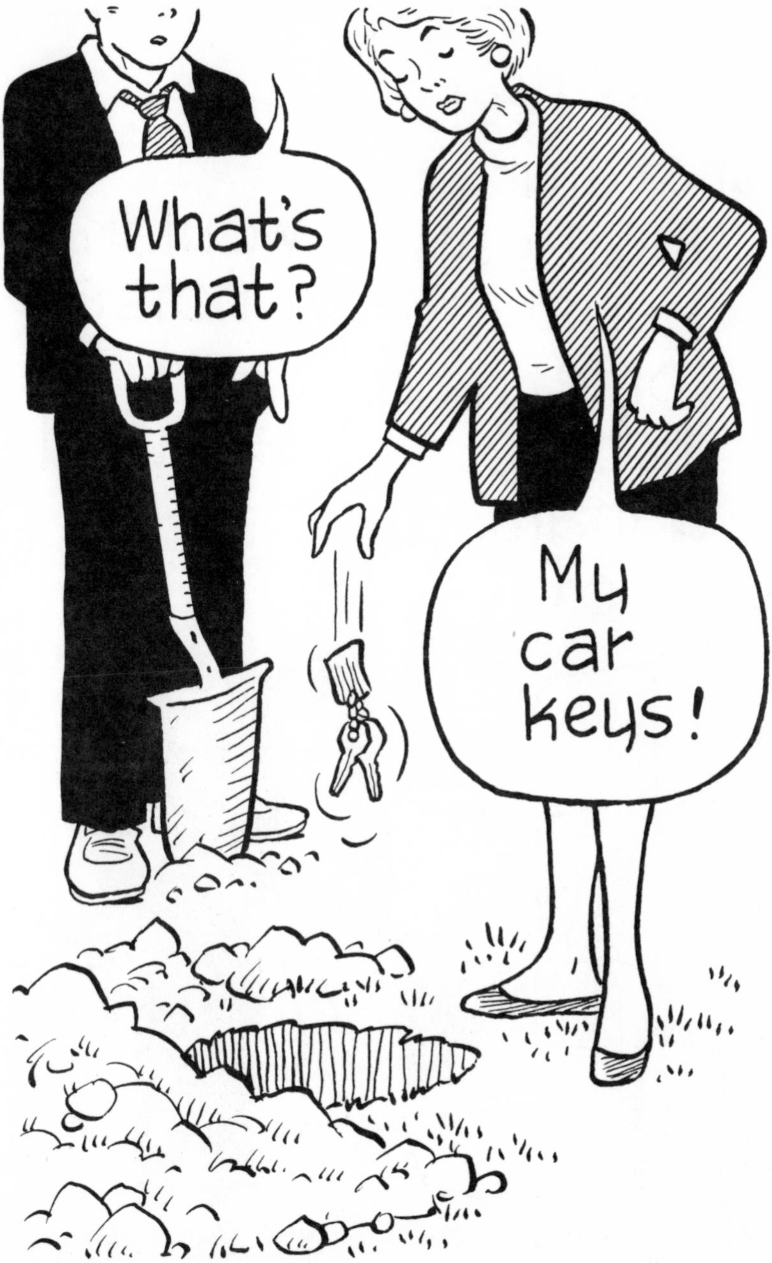
What's that?
My car keys!

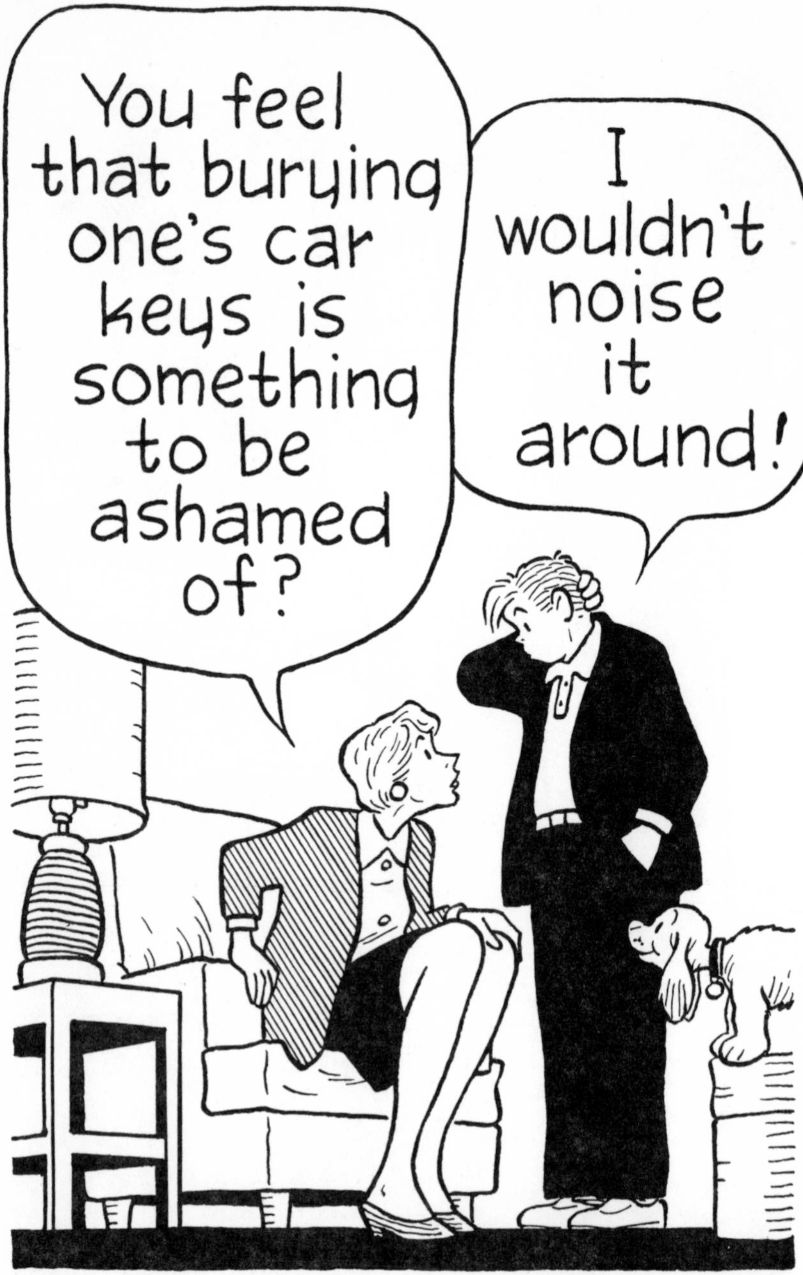
You feel that burying one's car keys is something to be ashamed of?
I wouldn't noise it around!

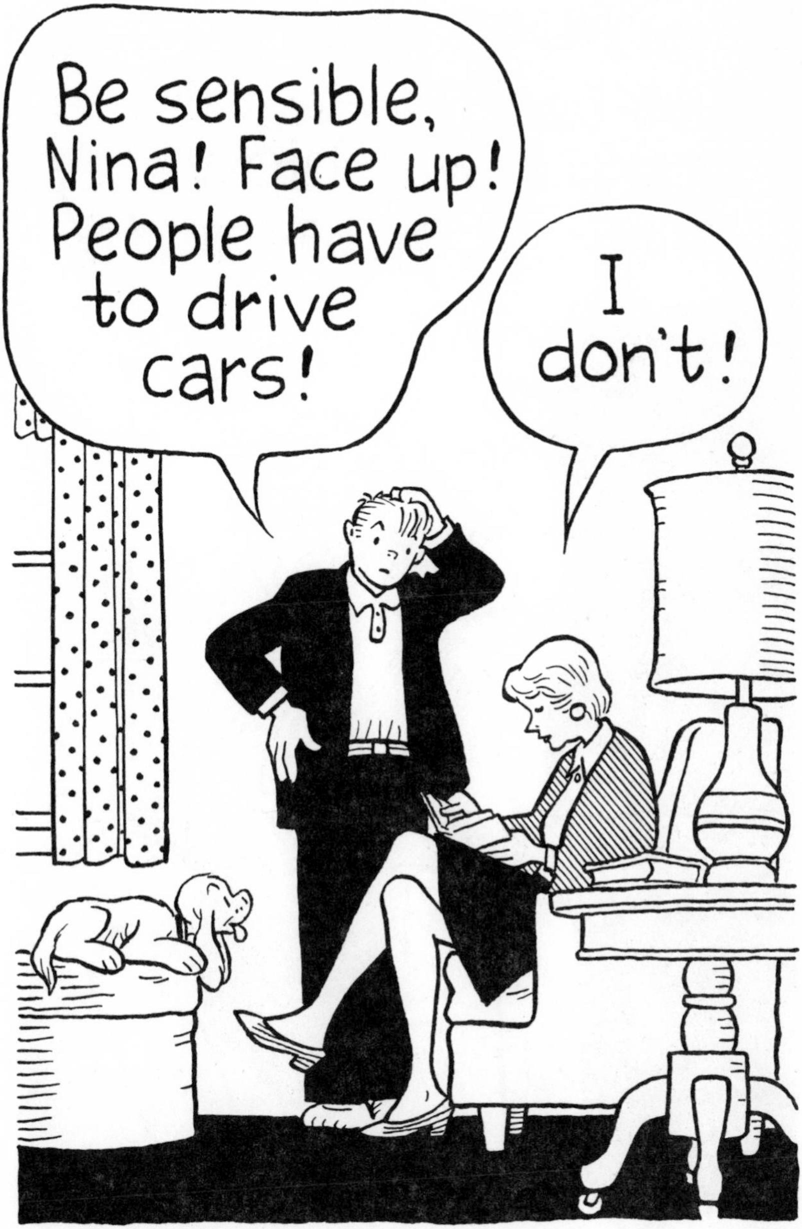
Be sensible, Nina! Face up! People have to drive cars!
I don't!

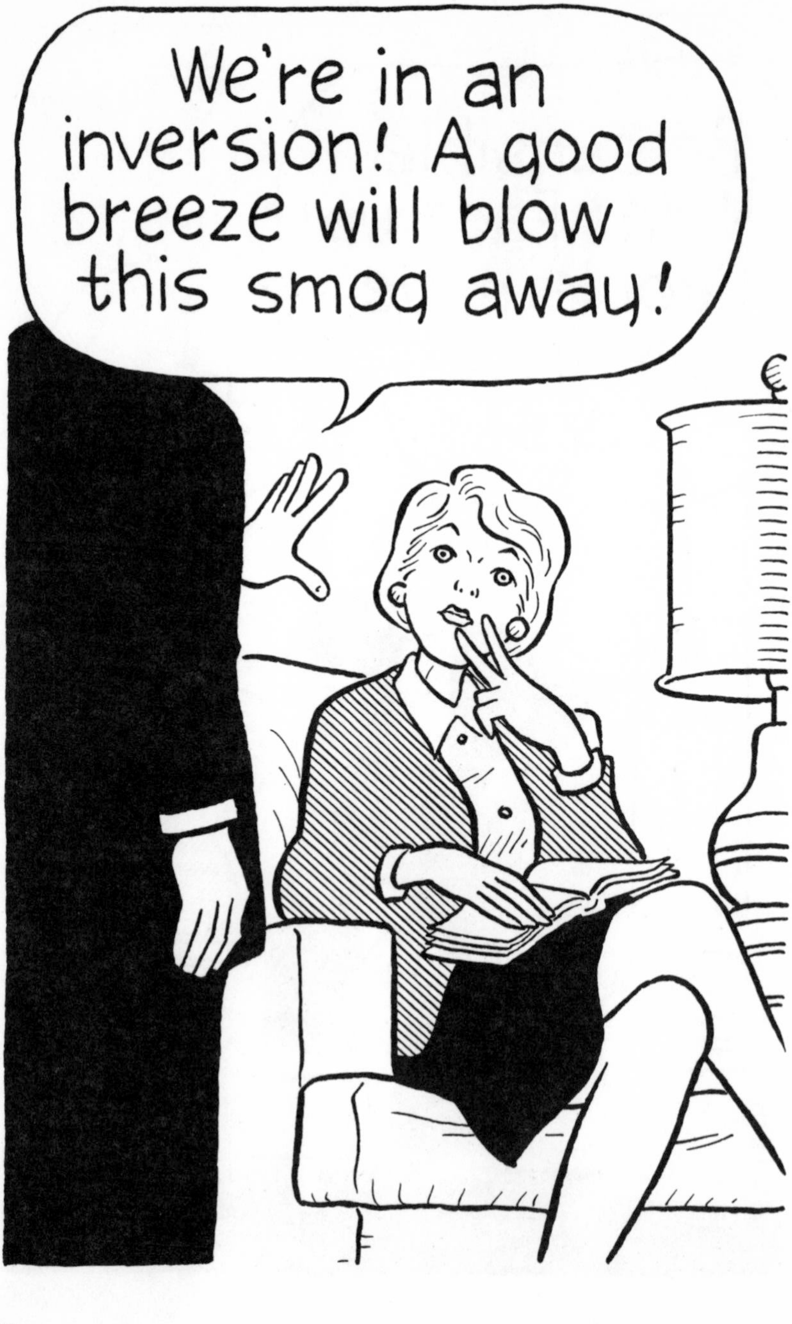
We're in an inversion! A good breeze will blow this smog away!

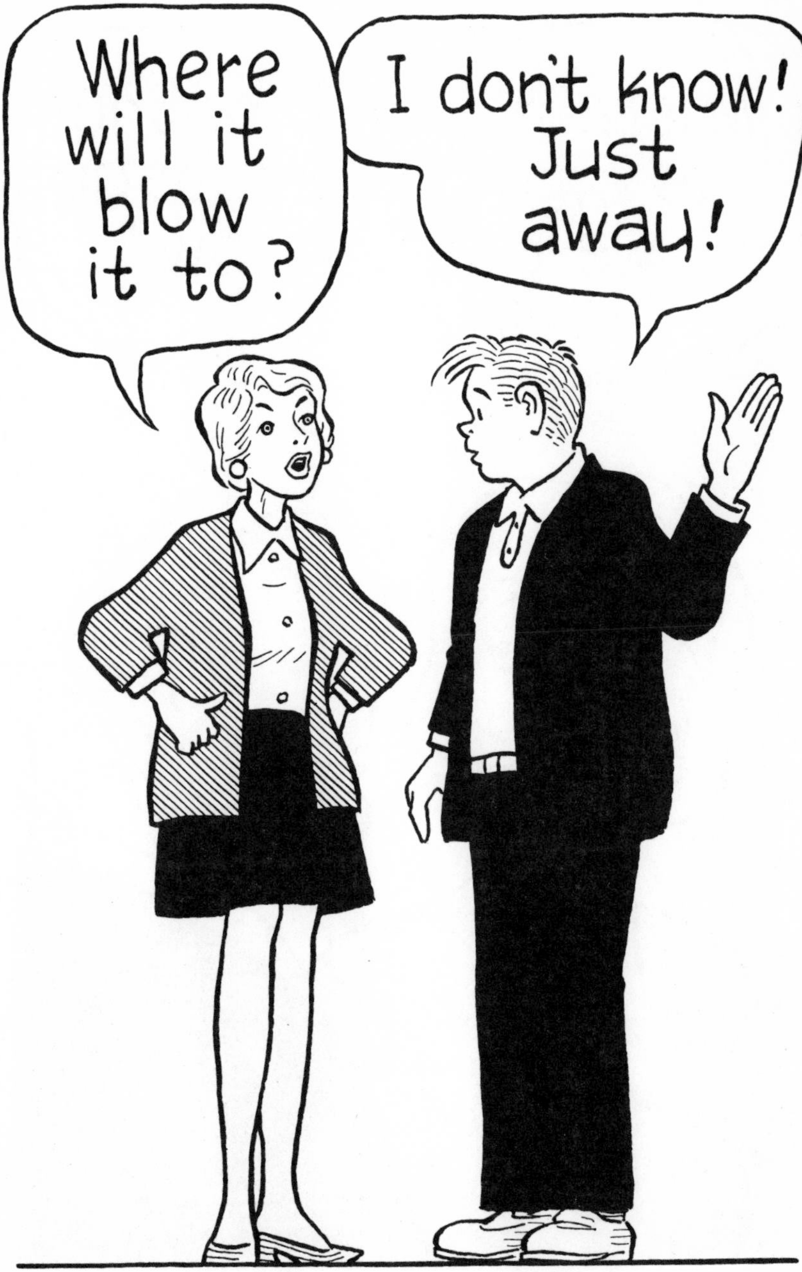
Where will it blow it to?
I don't know! Just away!

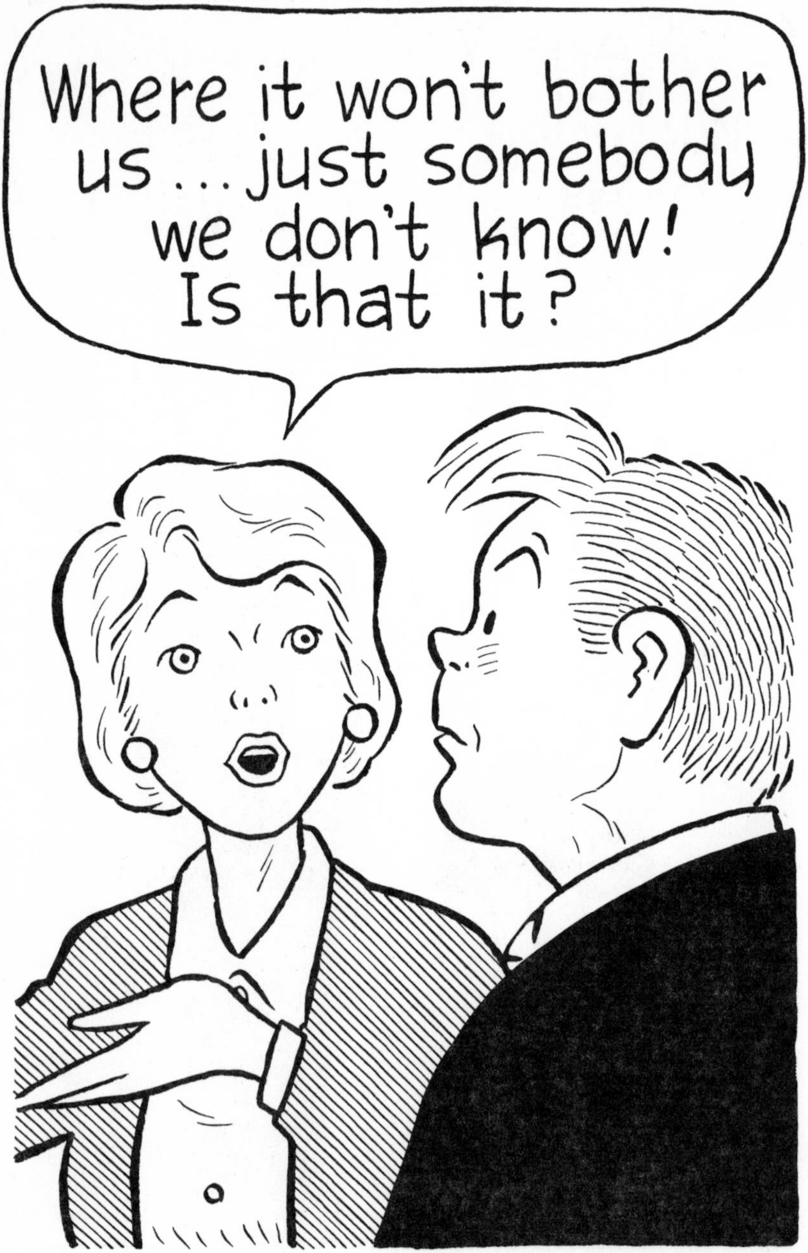
Where it won't bother us ... just somebody we don't know! Is that it?

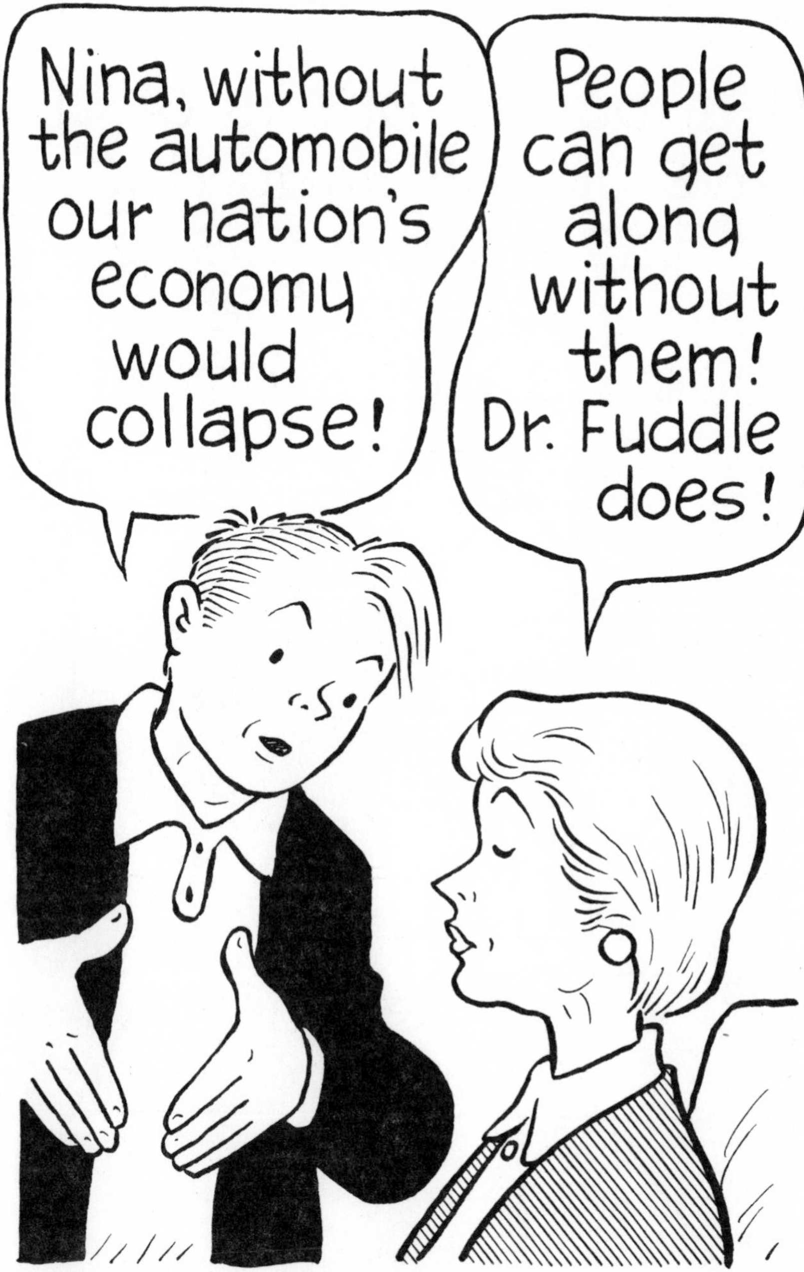
Nina, without the automobile our nation's economy would collapse!
People can get along without them! Dr. Fuddle does!

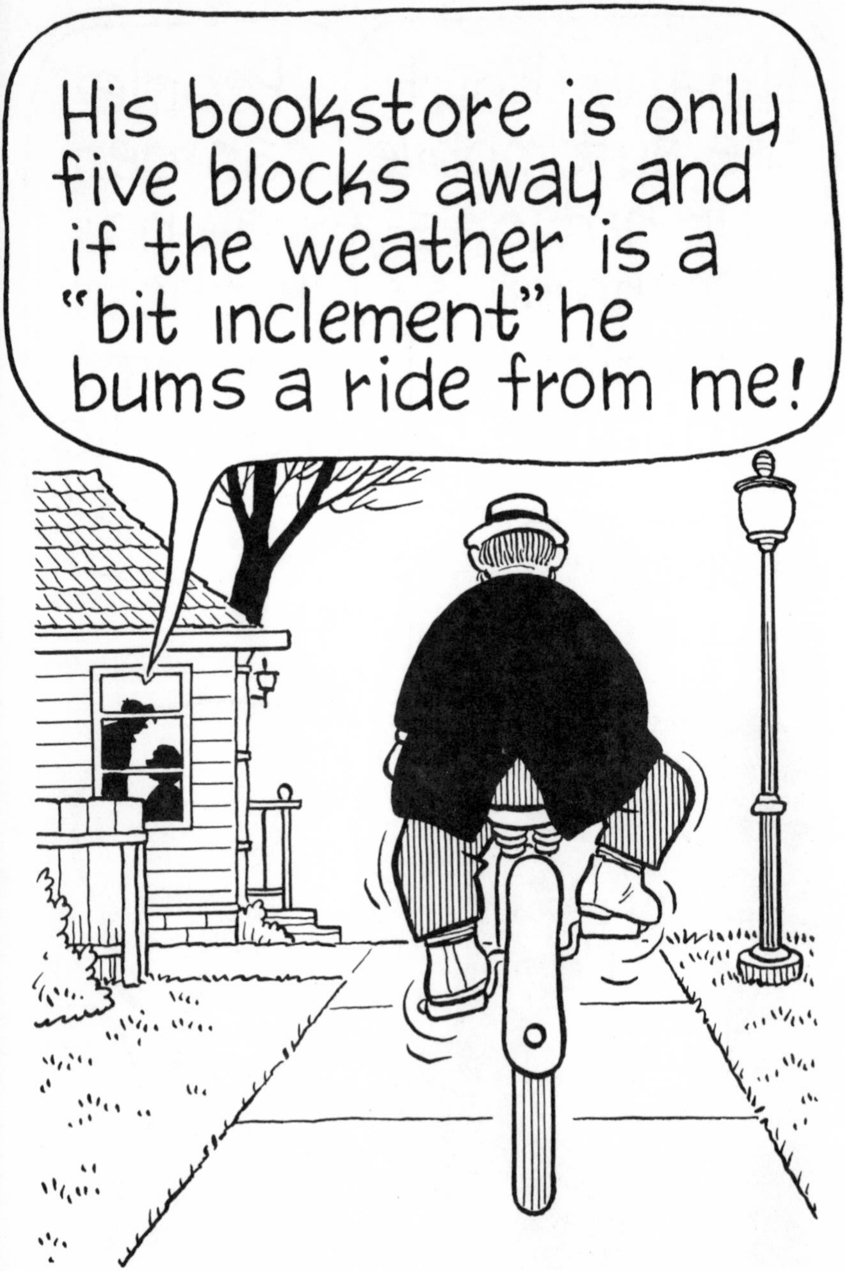
His bookstore is only five blocks away and if the weather is a "bit inclement" he bums a ride from me!

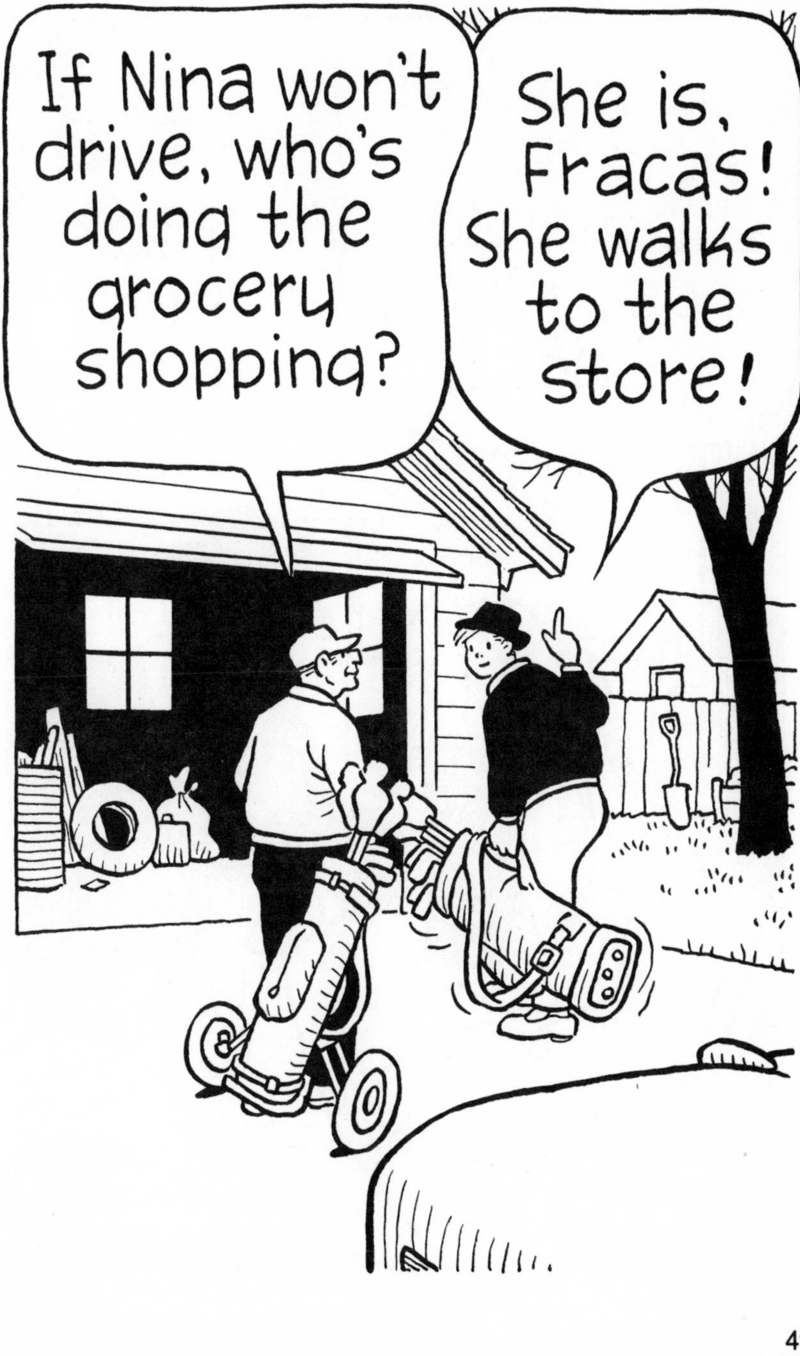
If Nina won't drive, who's doing the grocery shopping?
She is, Fracas! She walks to the store!

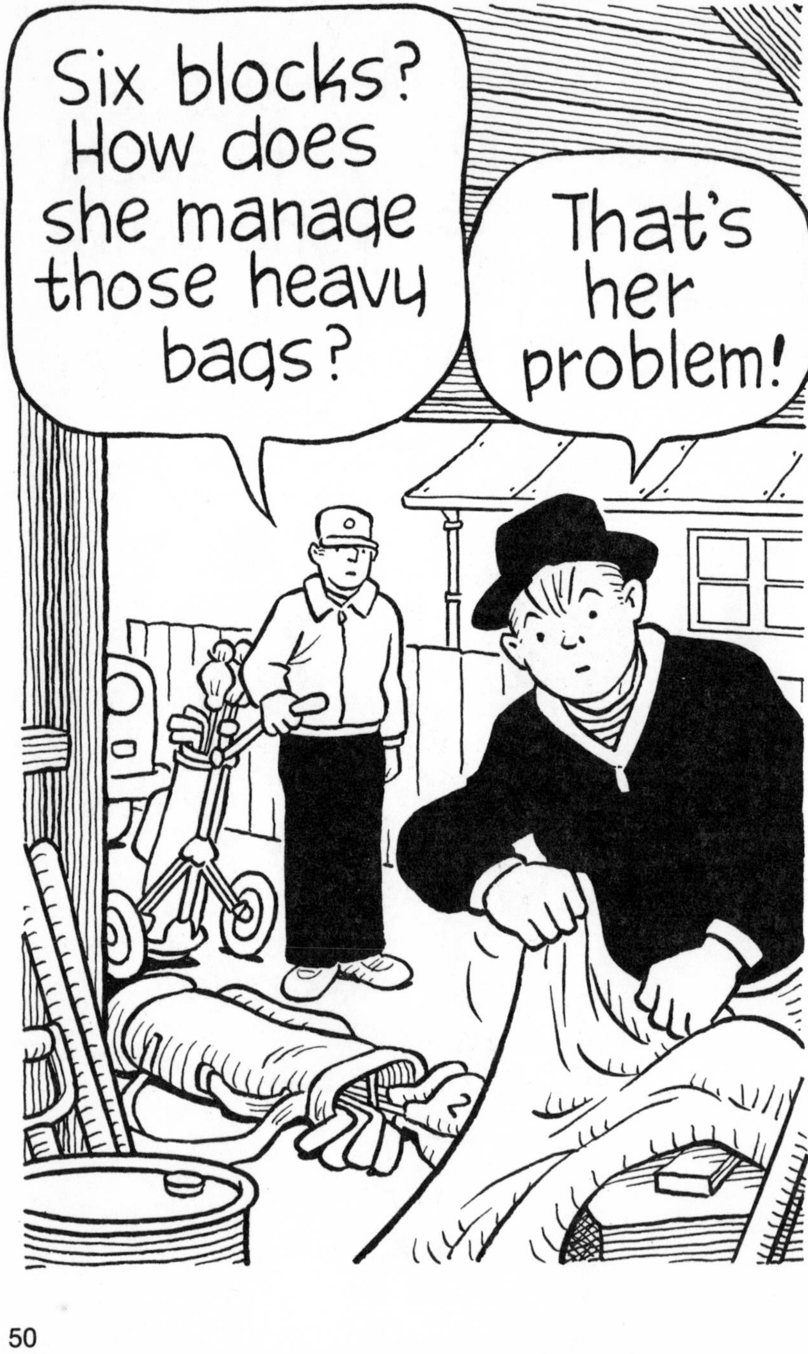
Six blocks? How does she manage those heavy bags?
That's her problem!

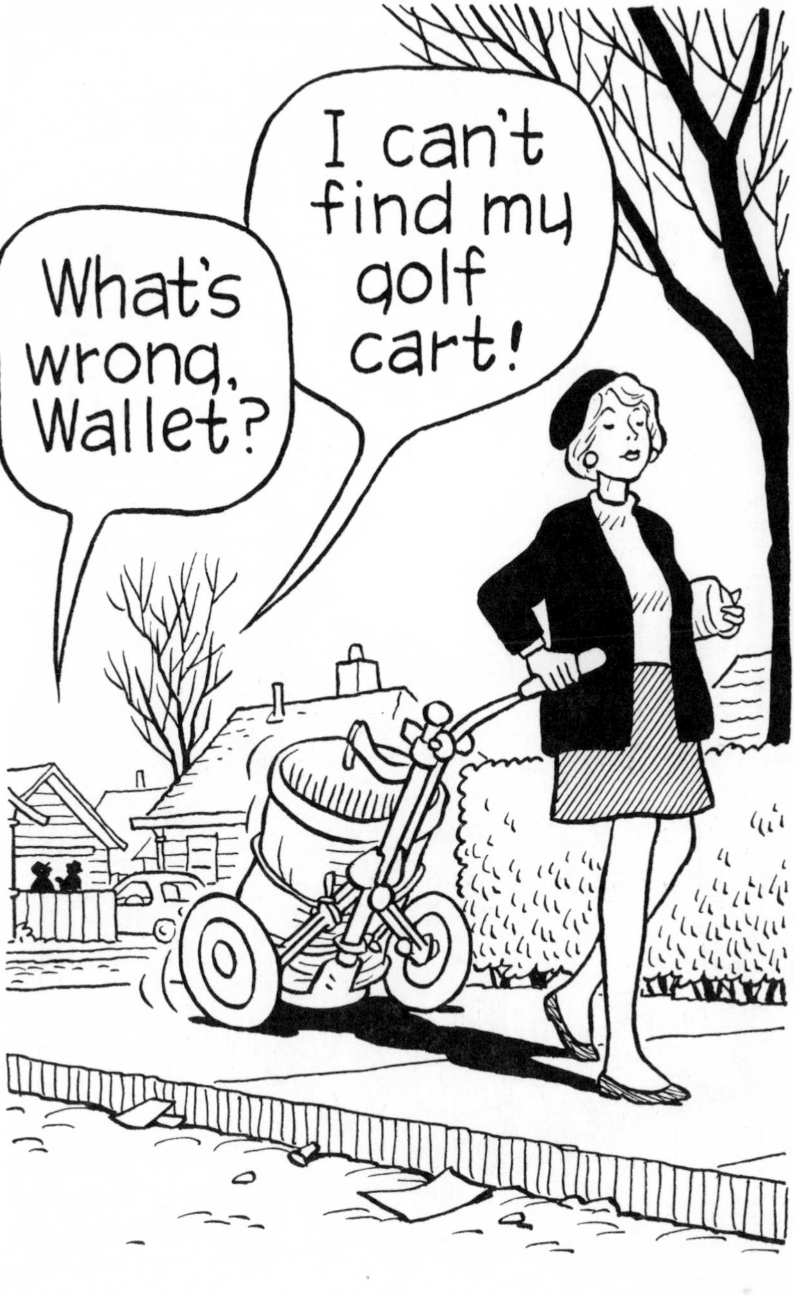
What's wrong, Wallet?
I can't find my golf cart!

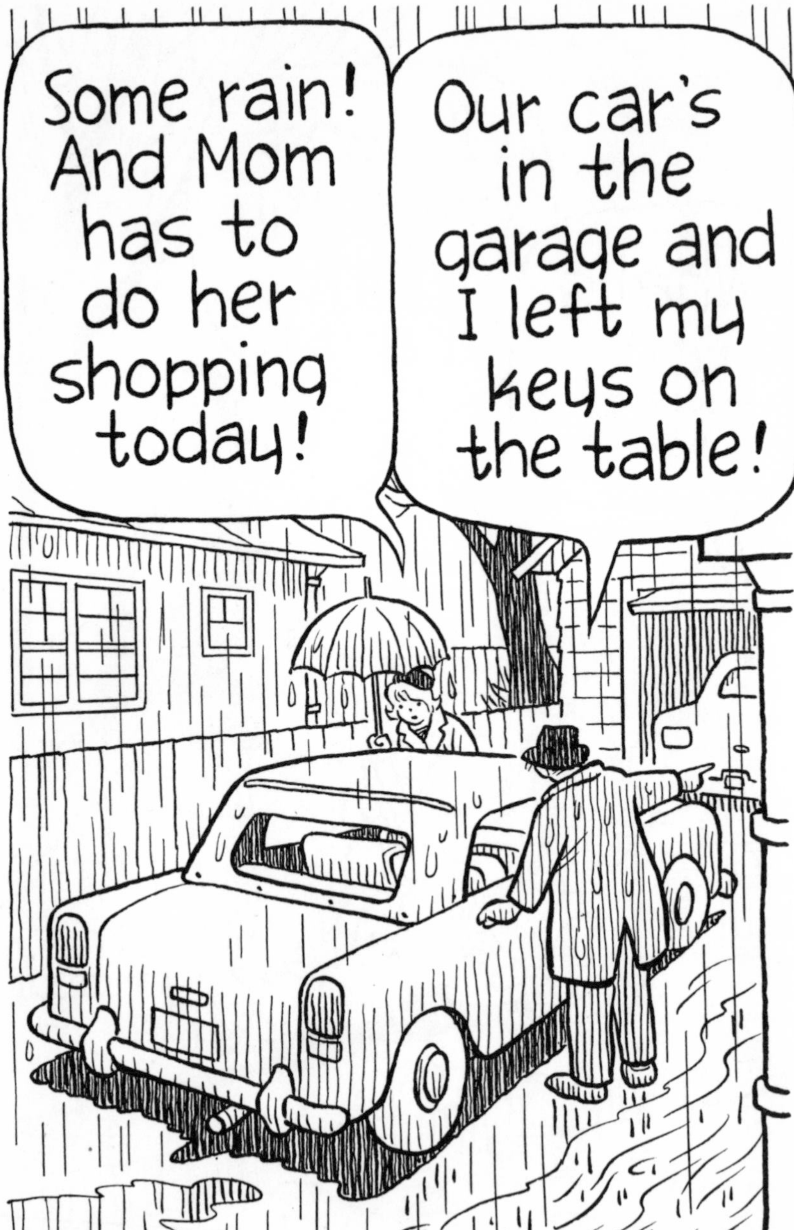
Some rain! And Mom has to do her shopping today!
Our car's in the garage and I left my keys on the table!

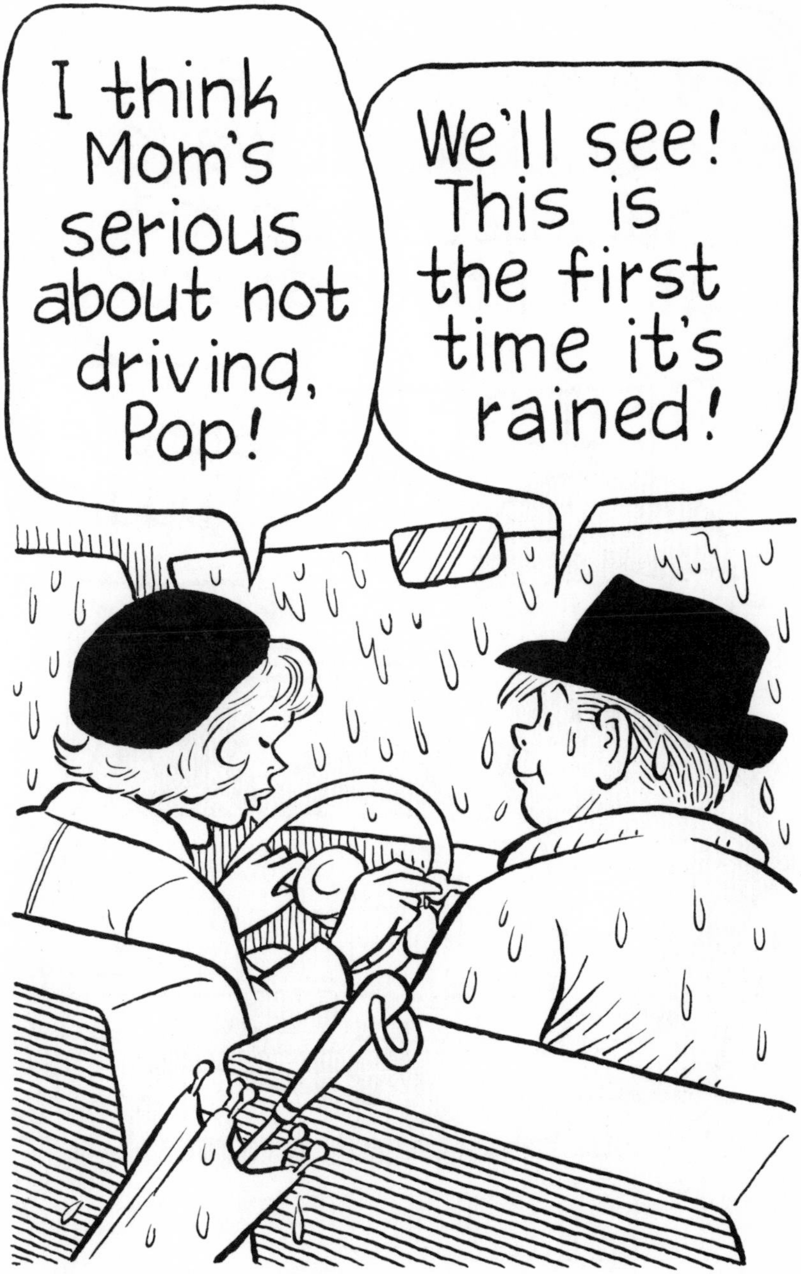
I think Mom's serious about not driving, Pop!
We'll see! This is the first time it's rained!

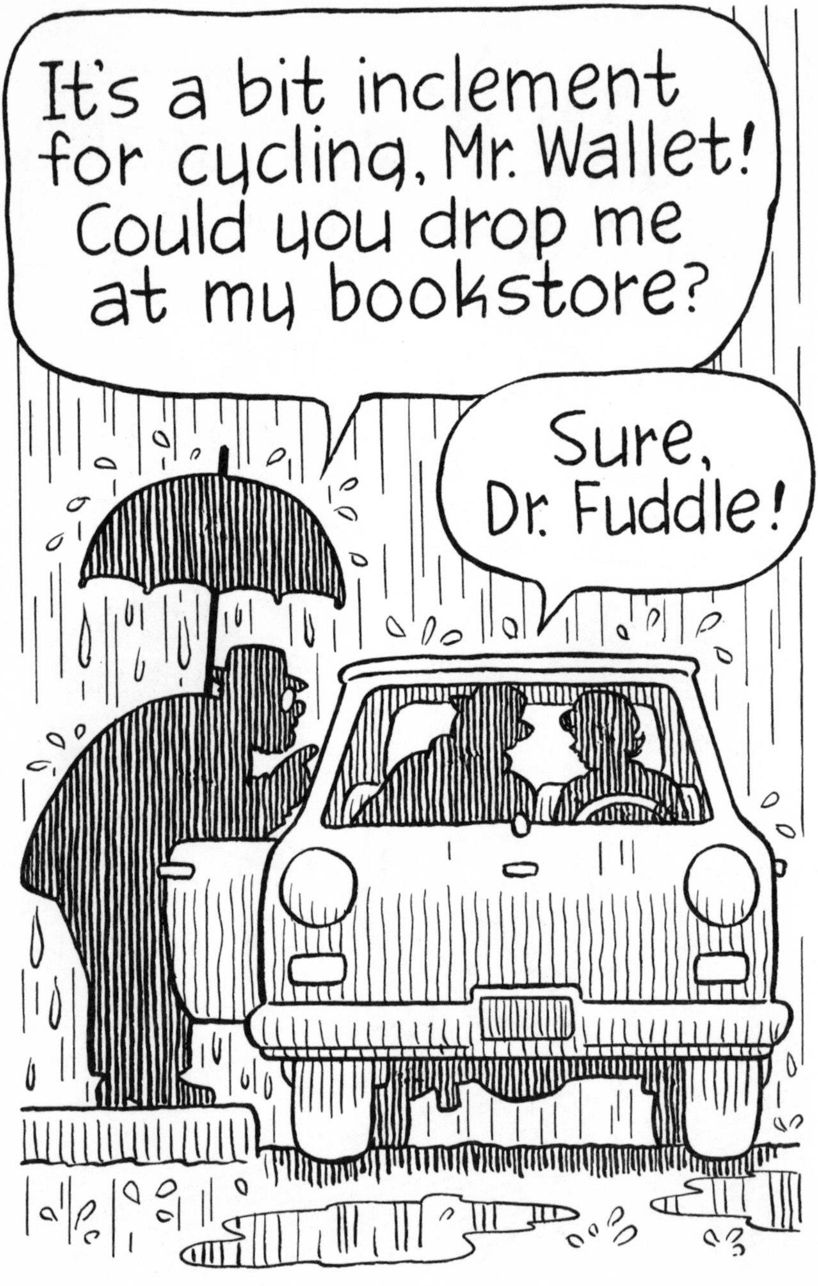
It's a bit inclement for cycling, Mr. Wallet! Could you drop me at my bookstore?
Sure, Dr. Fuddle!

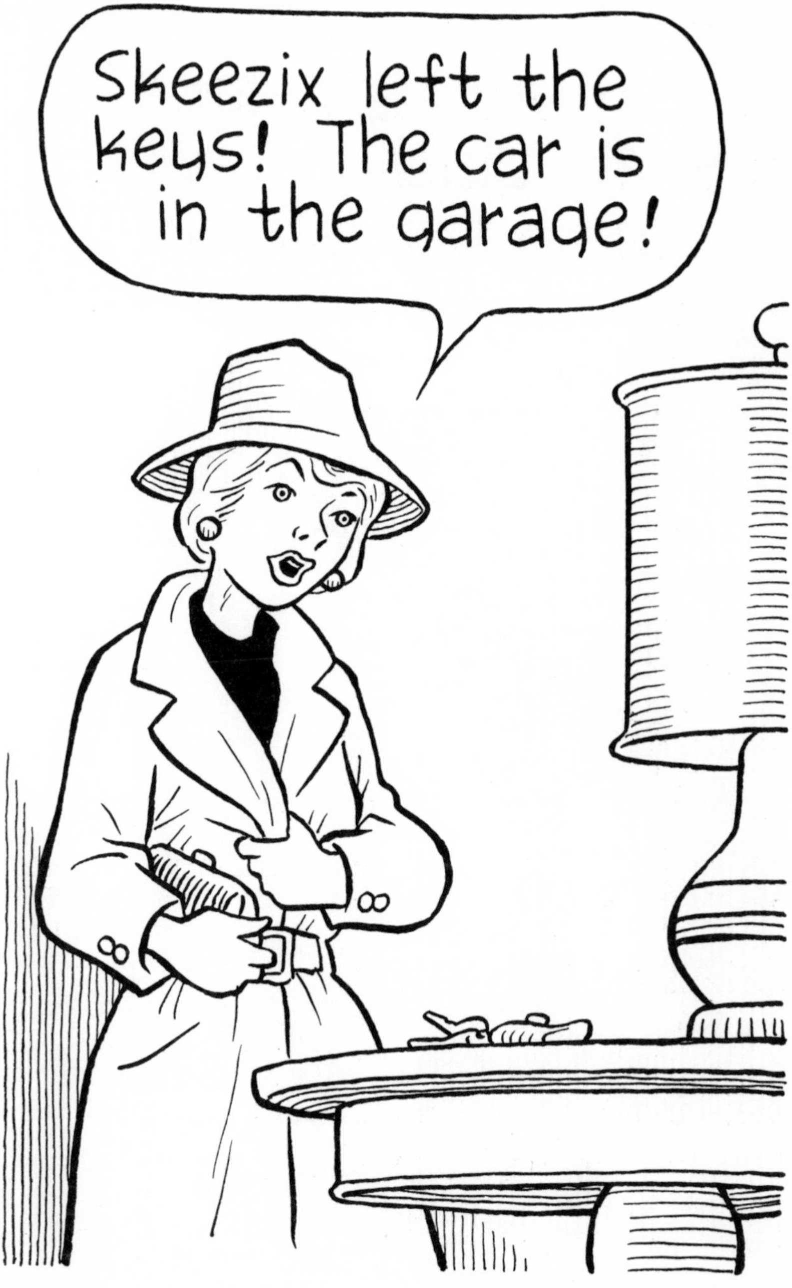
Skeezix left the keys! The car is in the garage!

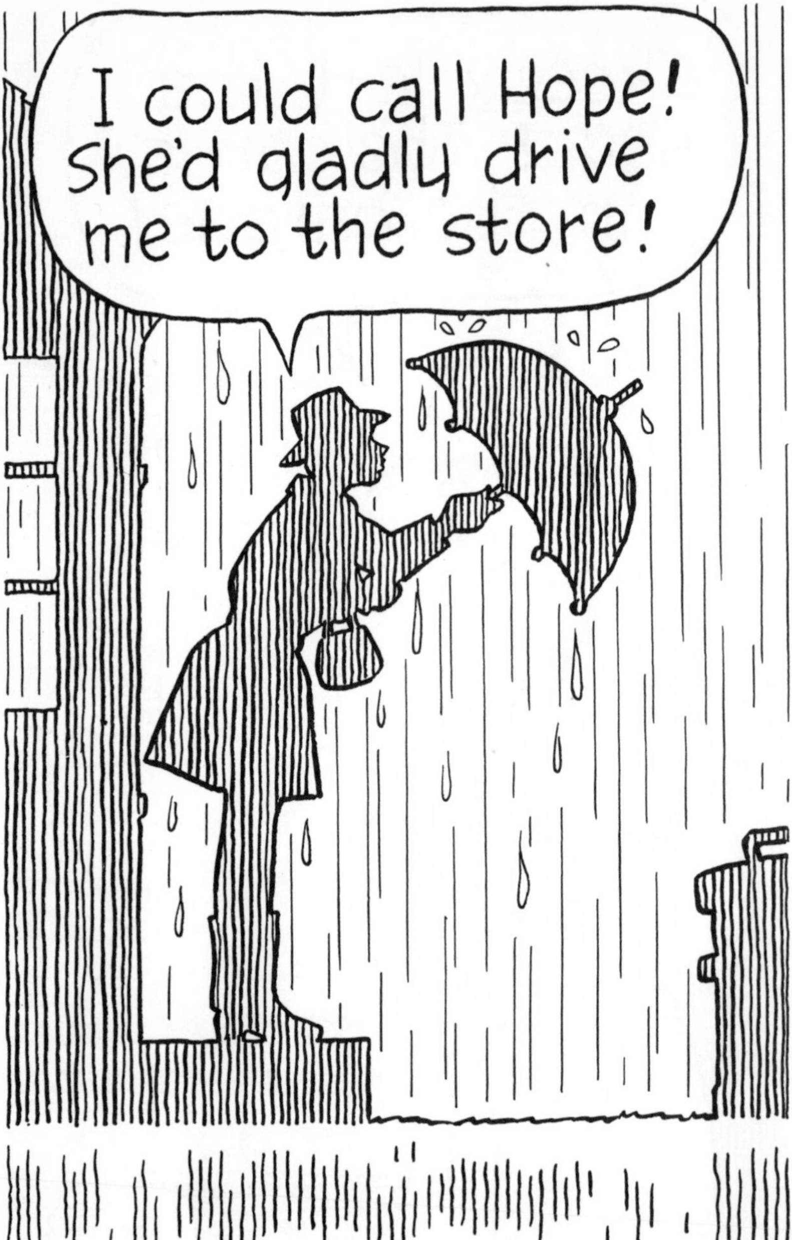
I could call Hope! She'd gladly drive me to the store!

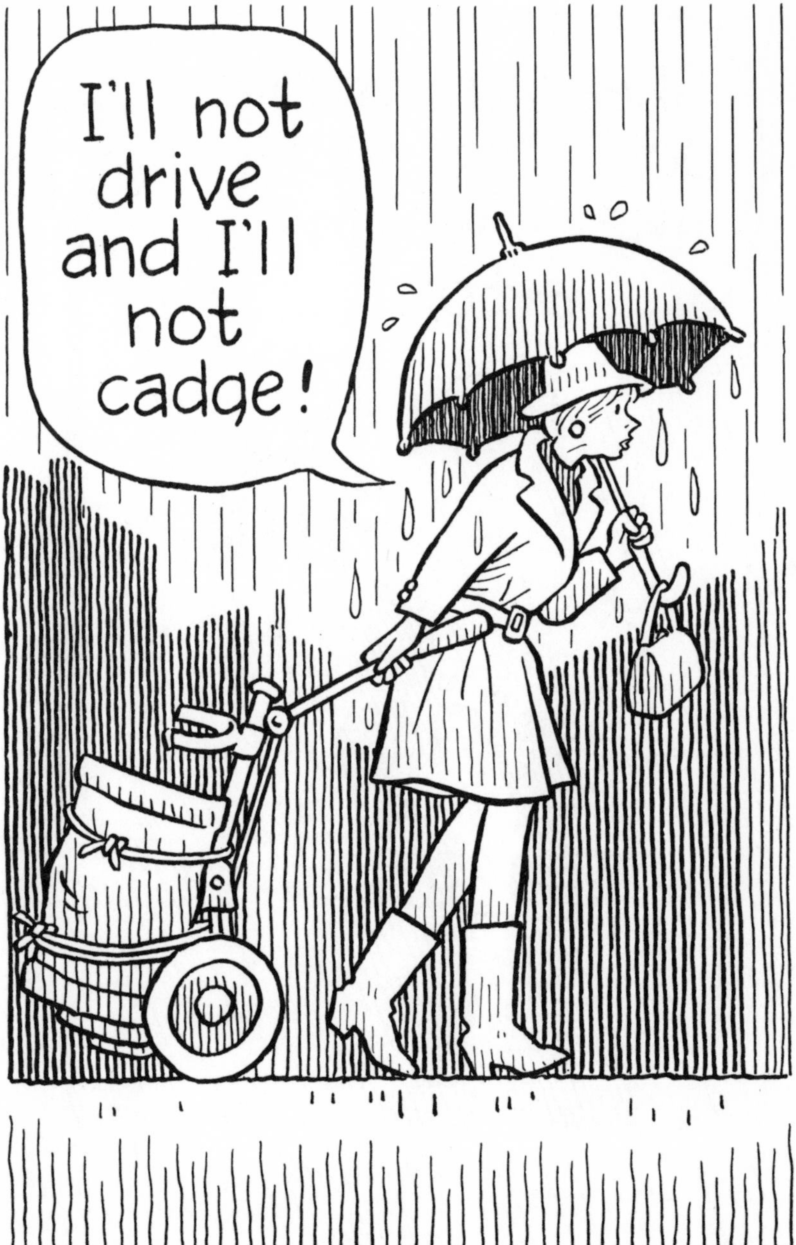
I'll not drive and I'll not cadge!

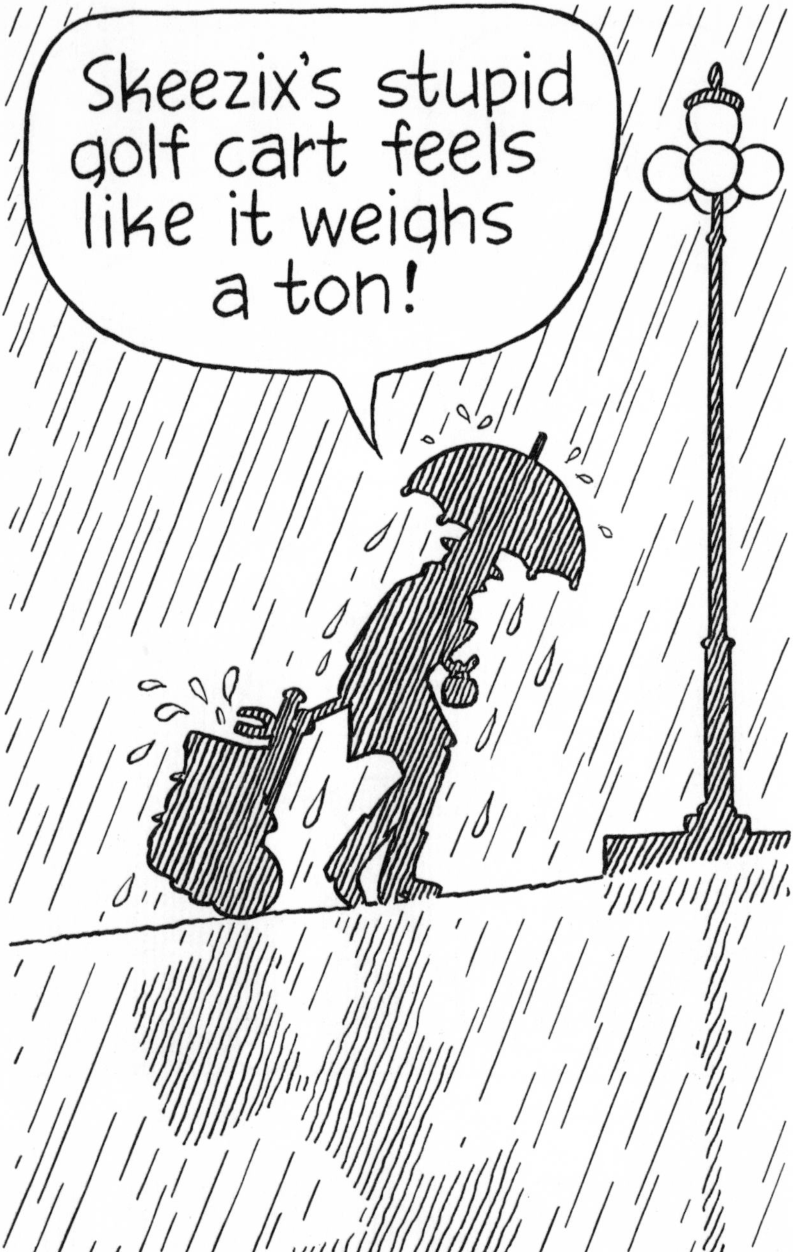
Skeezix's stupid golf cart feels like it weighs a ton!

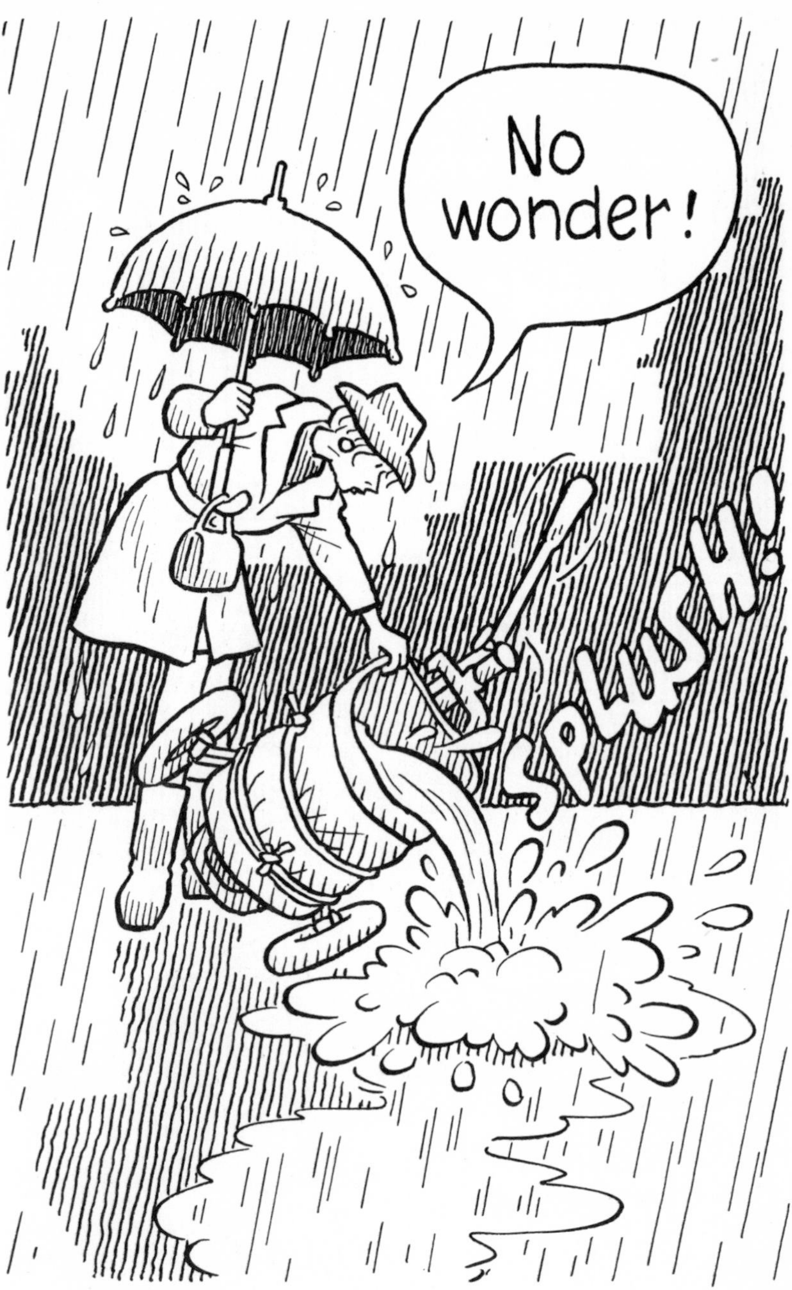
No wonder!
SPLUSH!

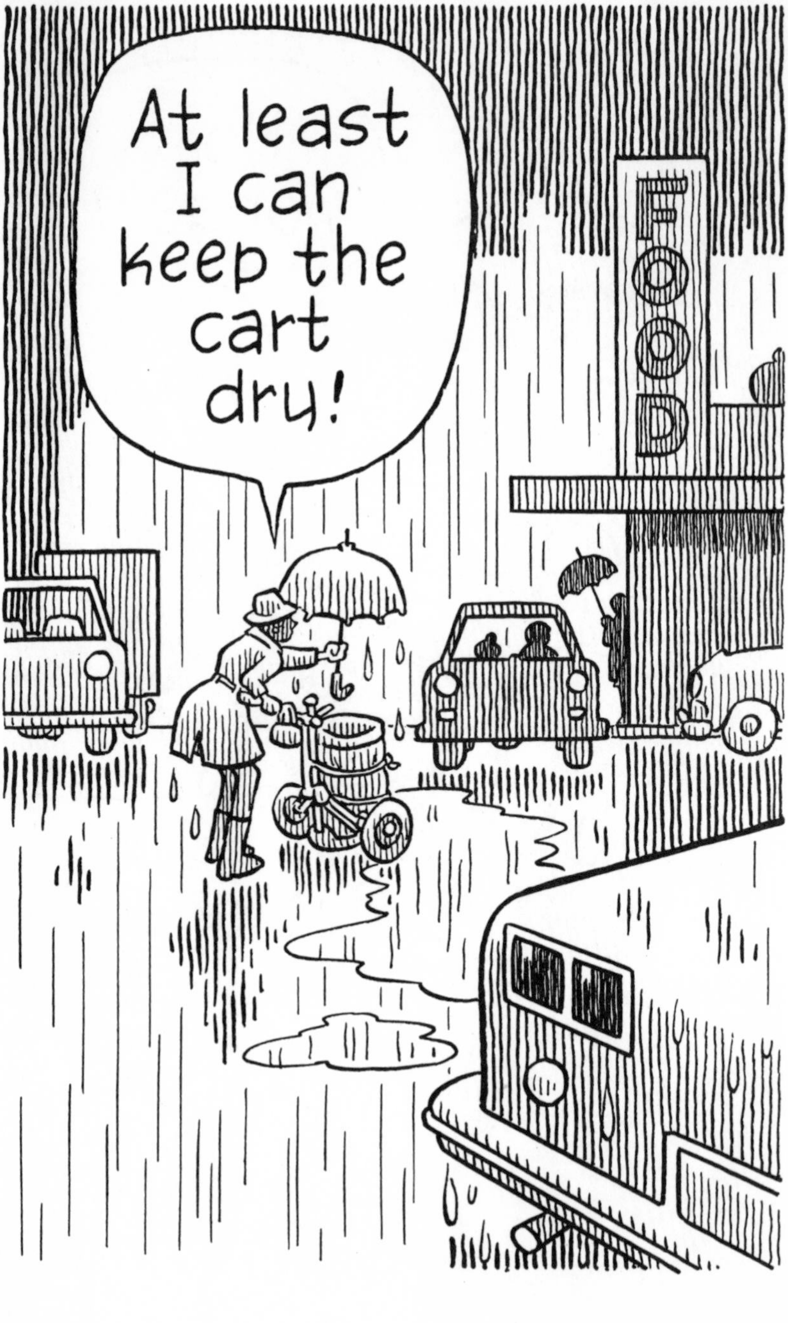
At least I can keep the cart dry!
FOOD

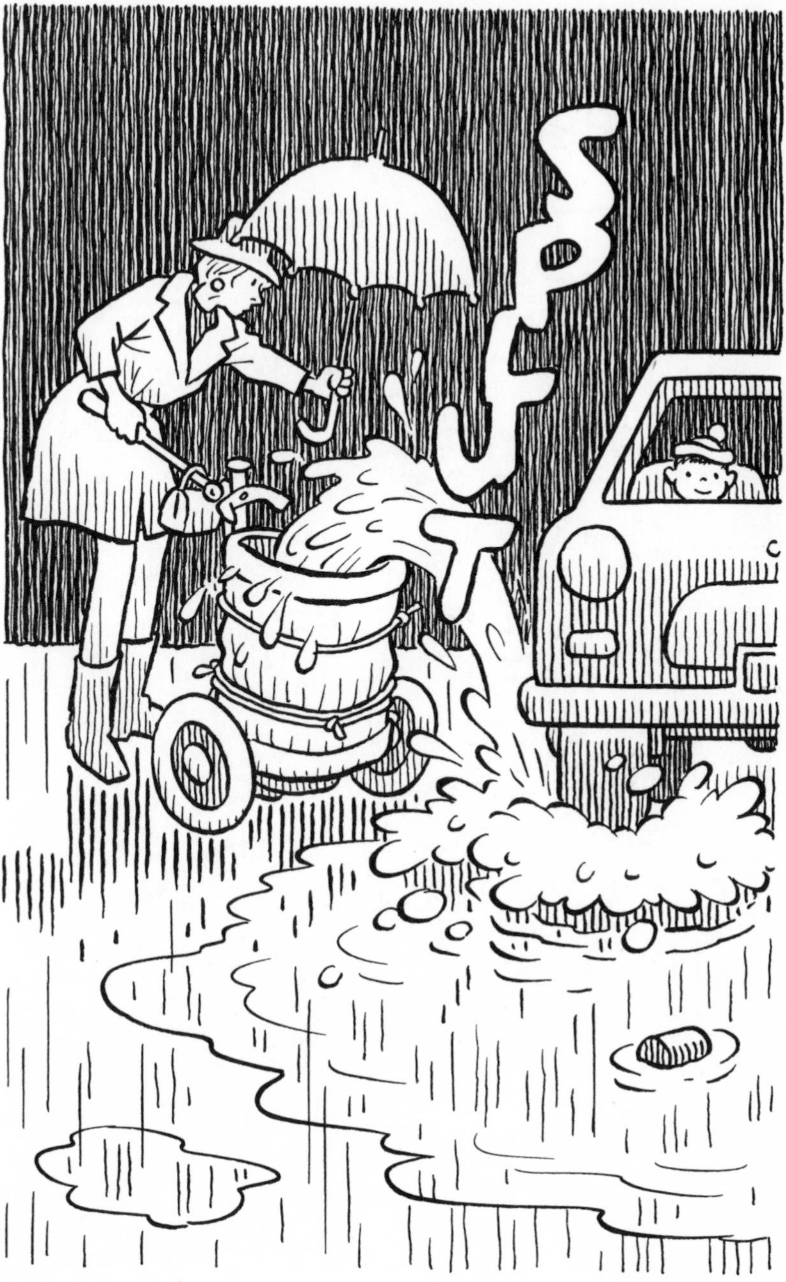
SPLUT

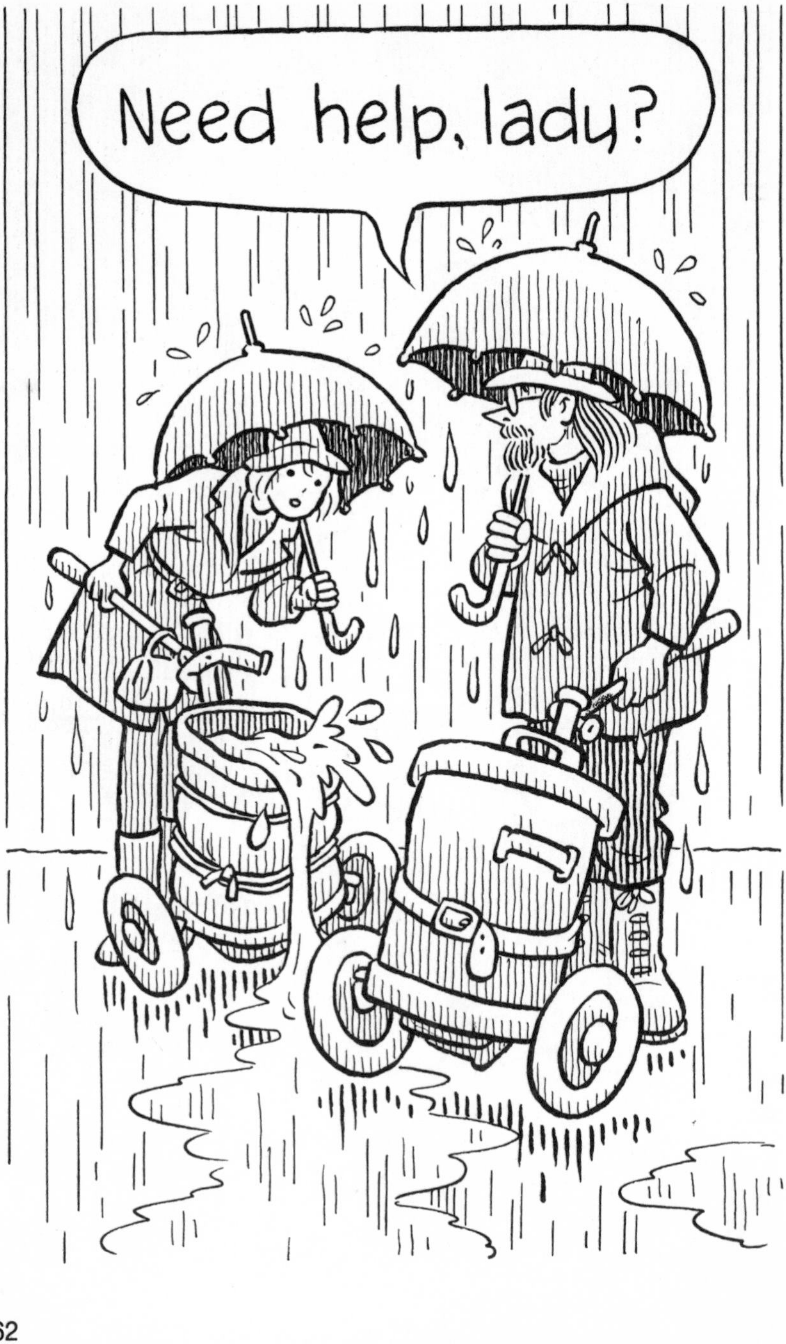
Need help, lady?

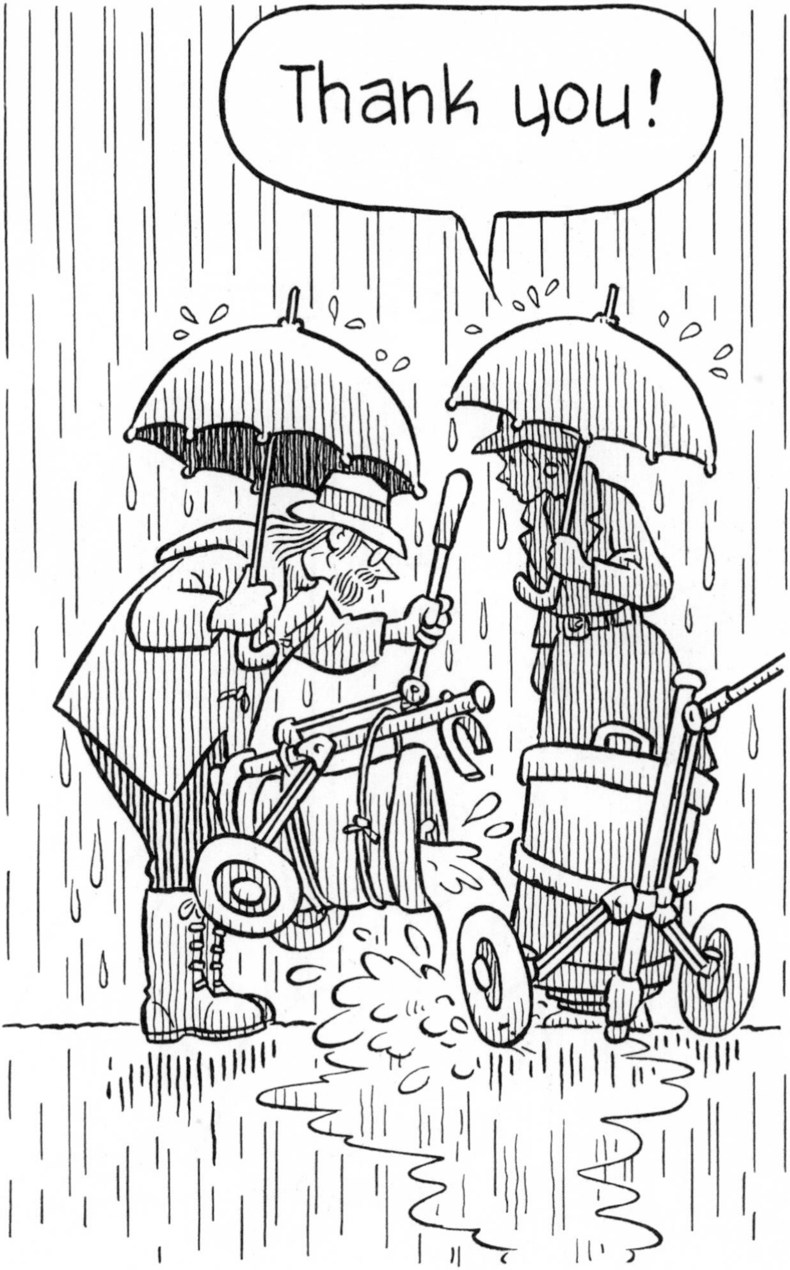
Thank you!

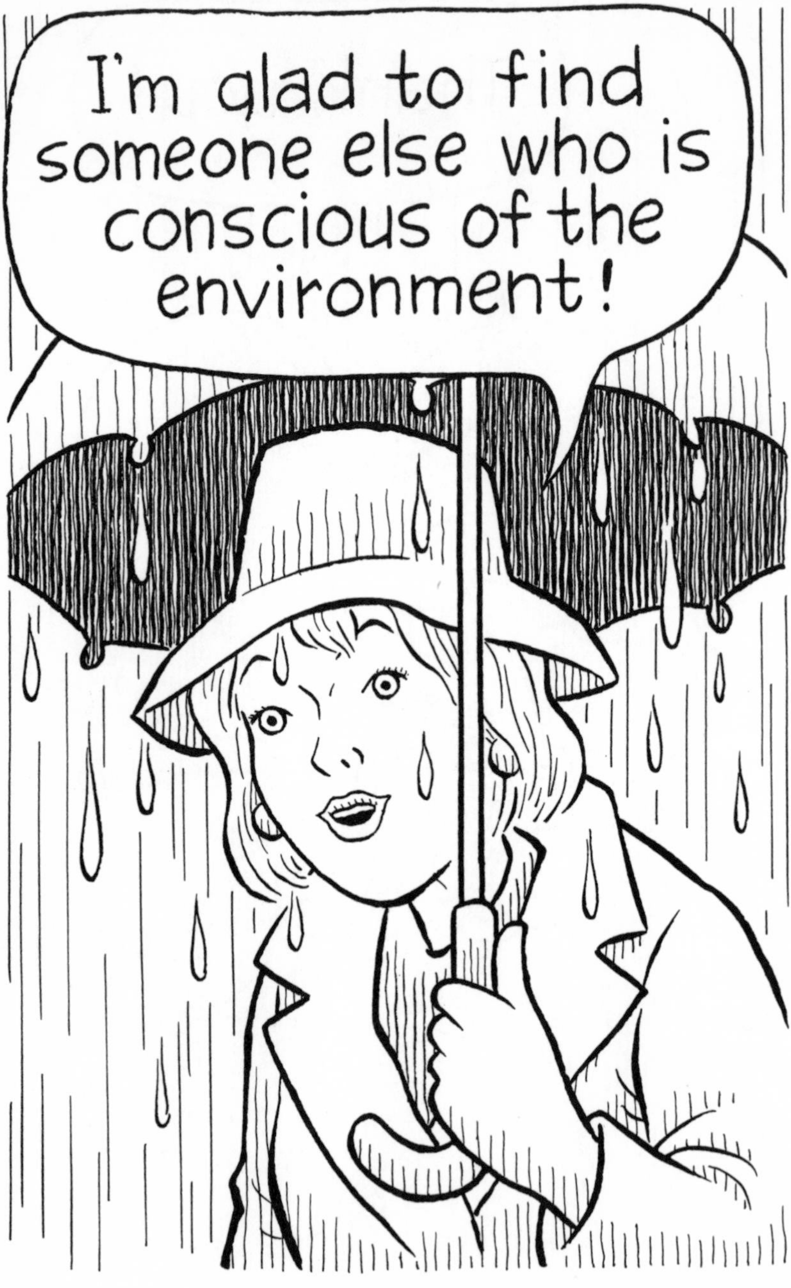
I'm glad to find someone else who is conscious of the environment!

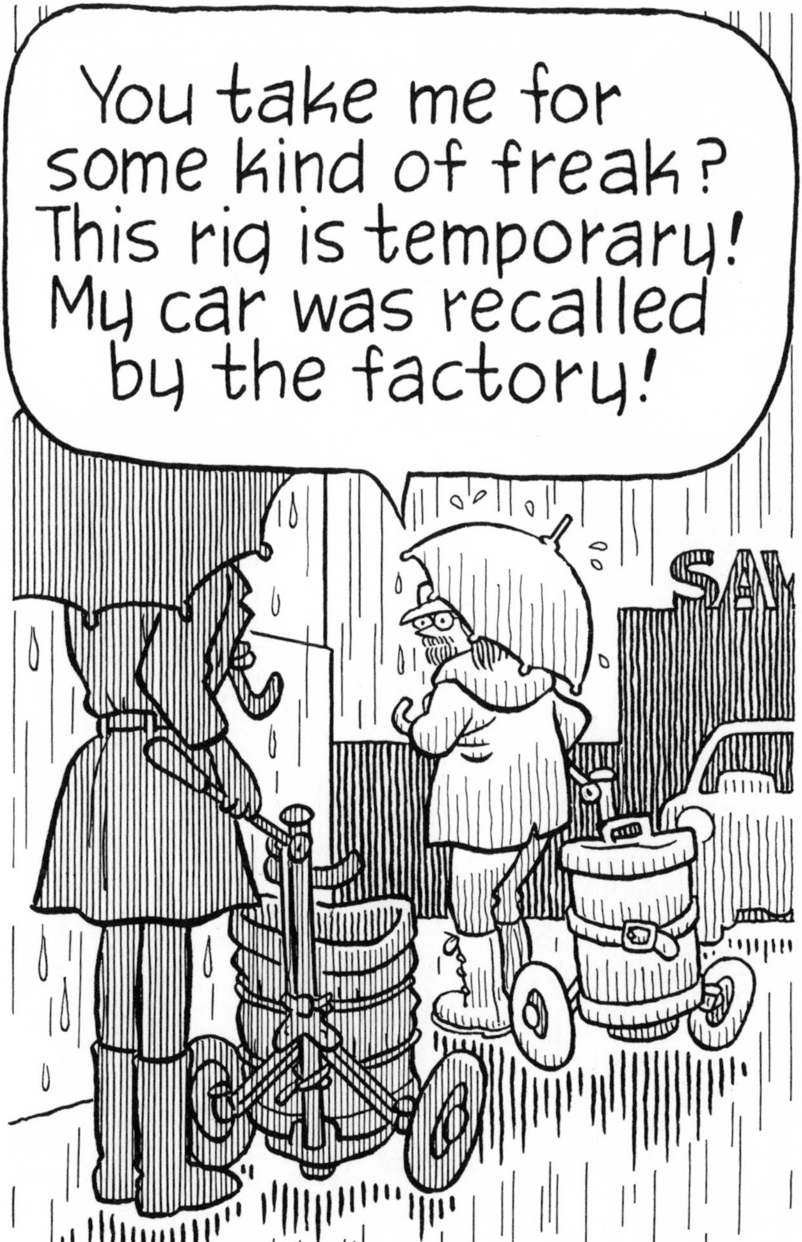
You take me for some kind of freak? This rig is temporary! My car was recalled by the factory!
SA

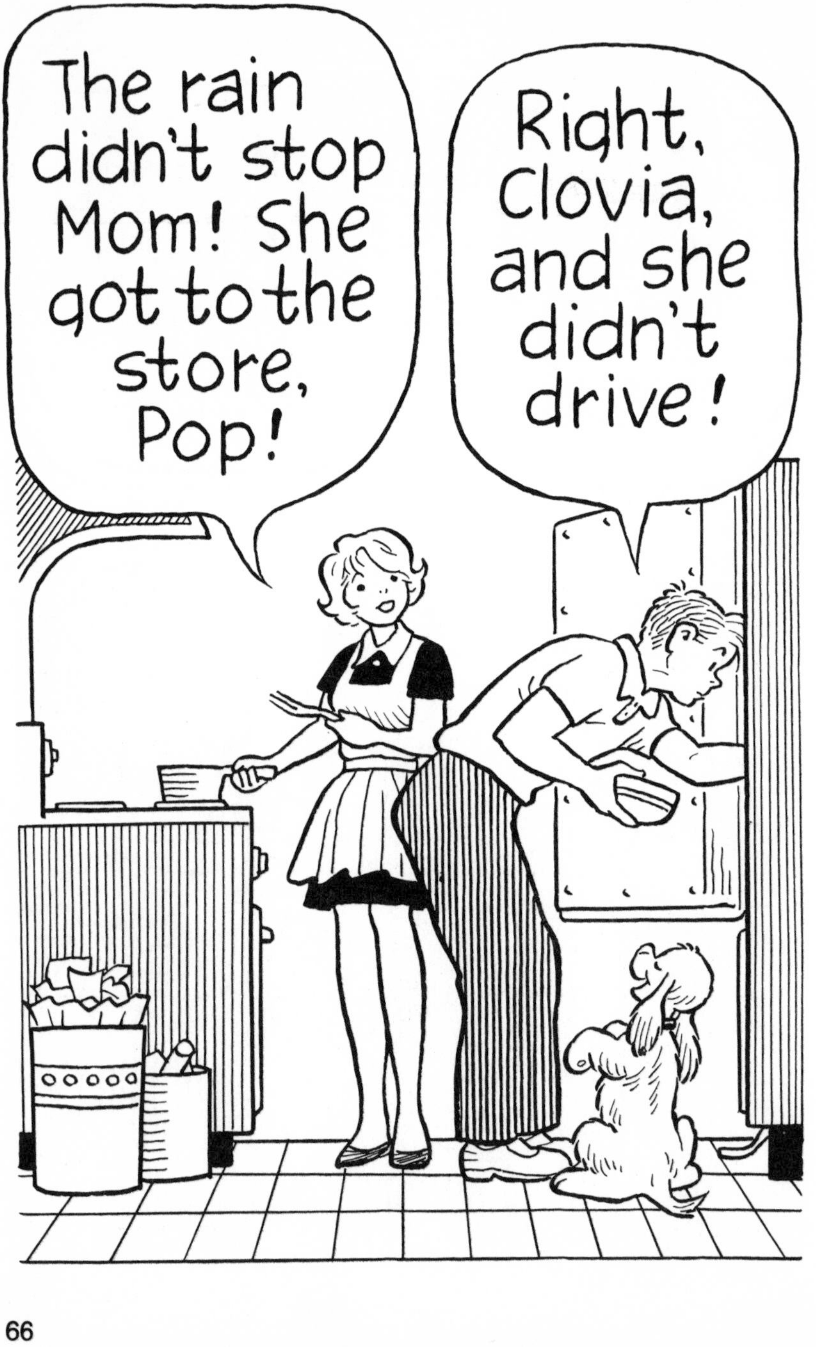
The rain didn't stop Mom! She got to the store, Pop!
Right, Clovia, and she didn't drive!

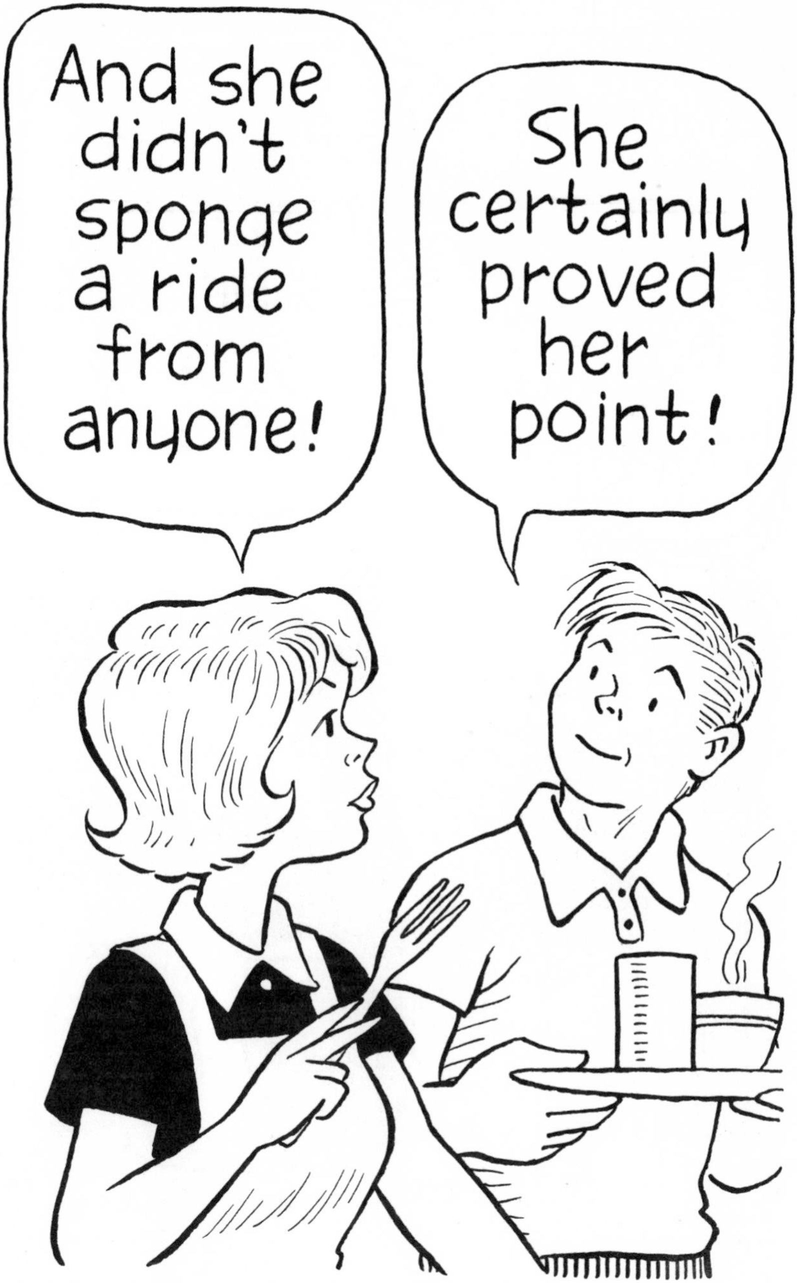
And she didn't sponge a ride from anyone!
She certainly proved her point!

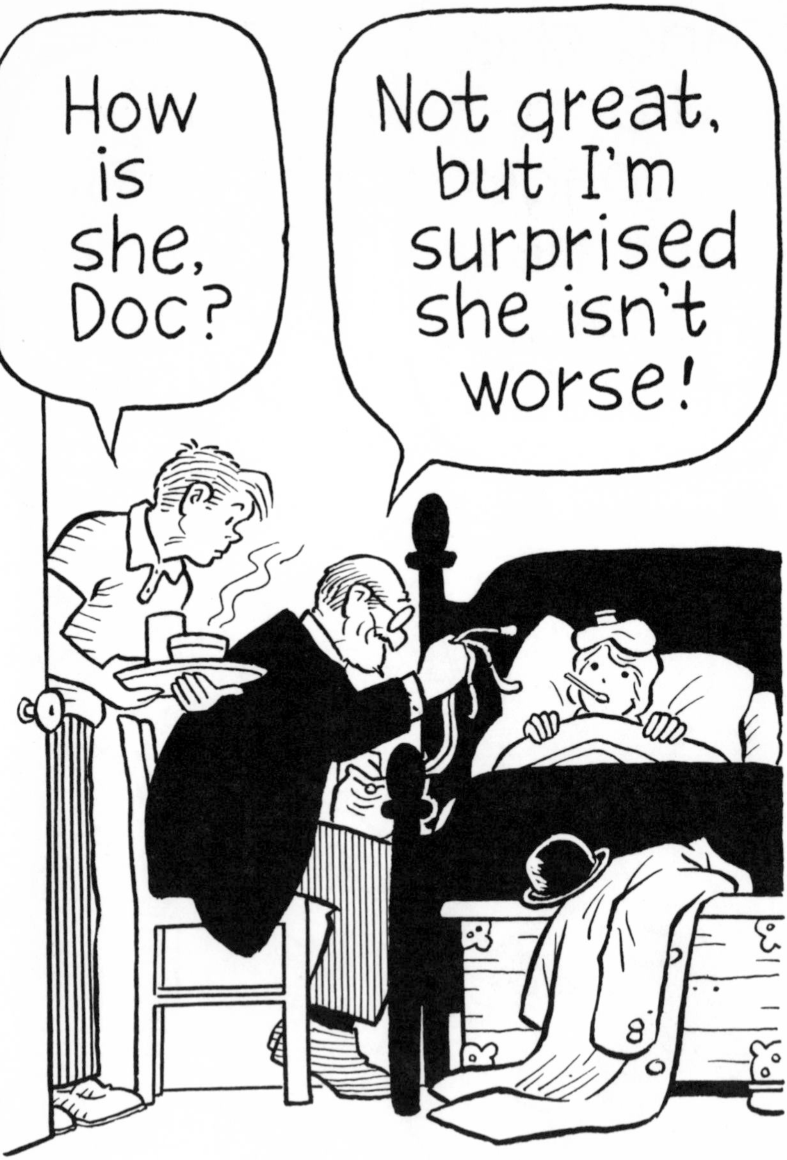
How is she, Doc?
Not great, but I'm surprised she isn't worse!

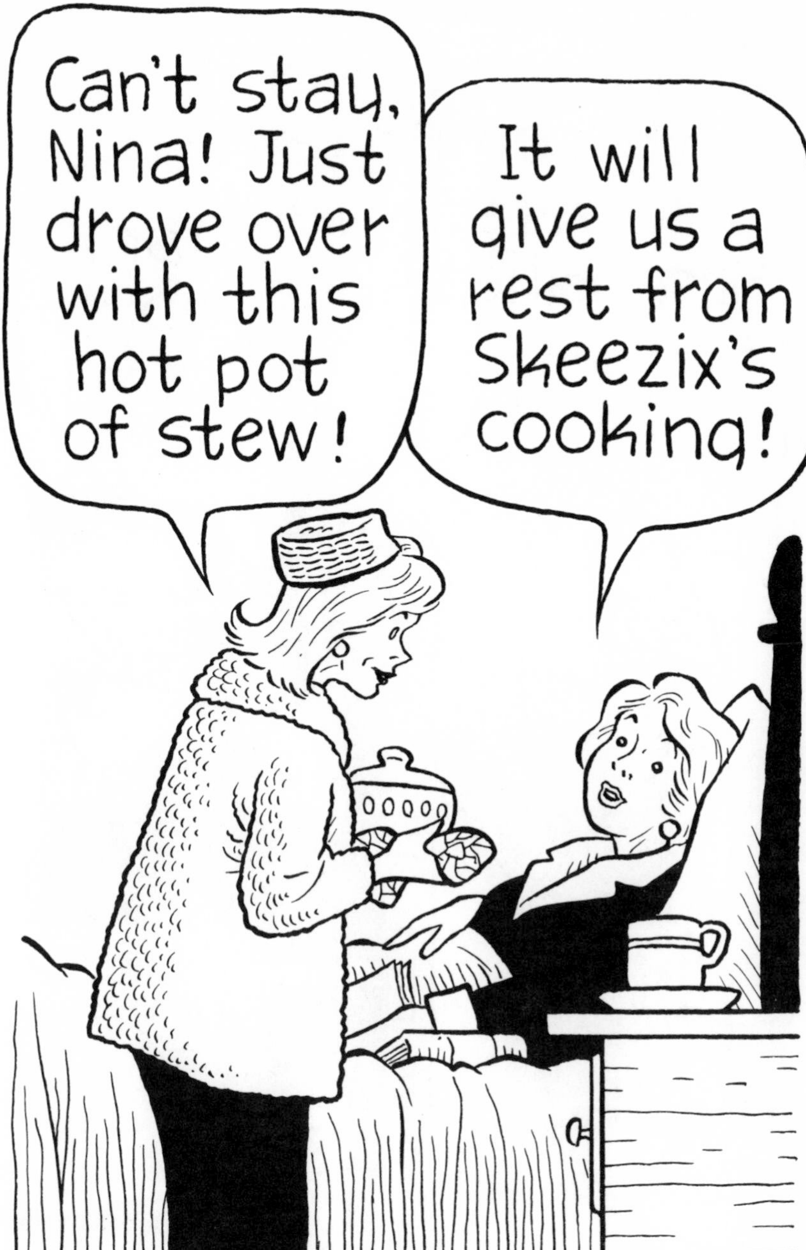
Can't stay, Nina! Just drove over with this hot pot of stew!
It will give us a rest from Skeezix's cooking!

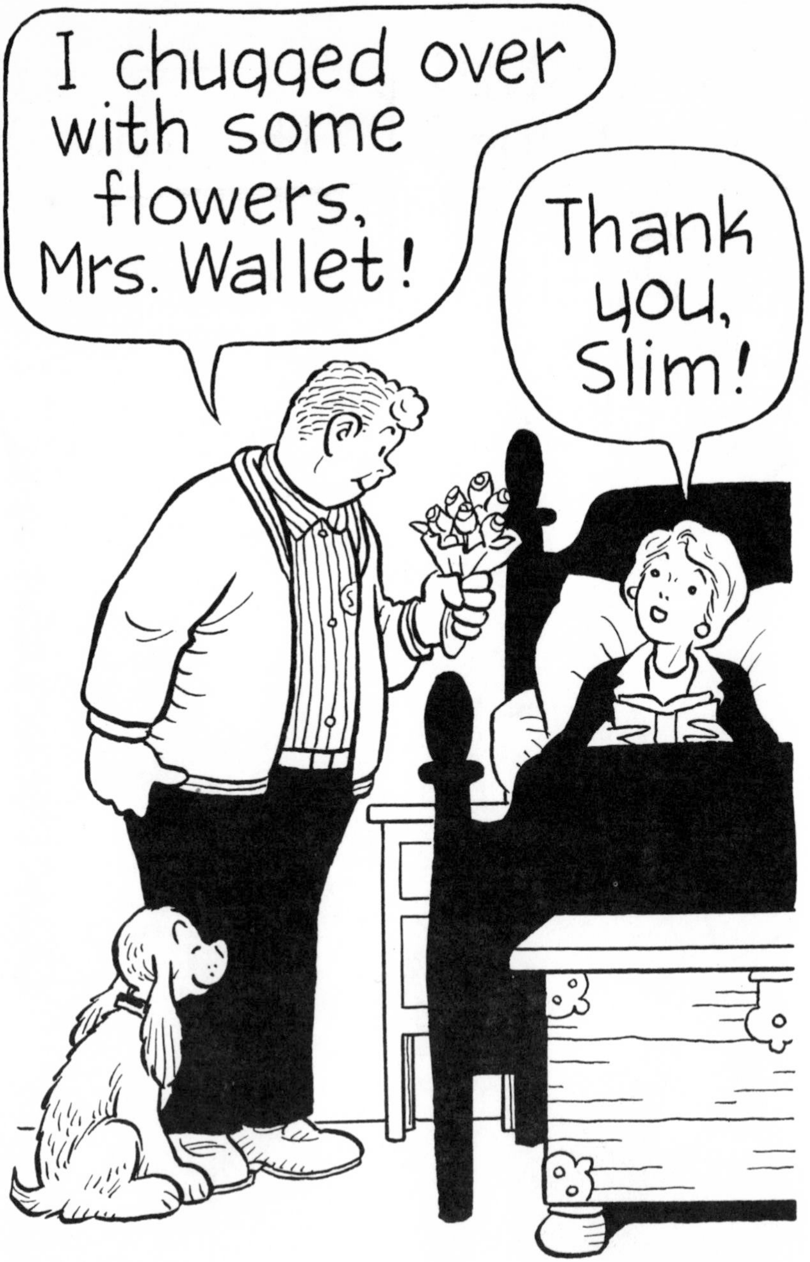
I chugged over with some flowers, Mrs. Wallet!
Thank you, Slim!

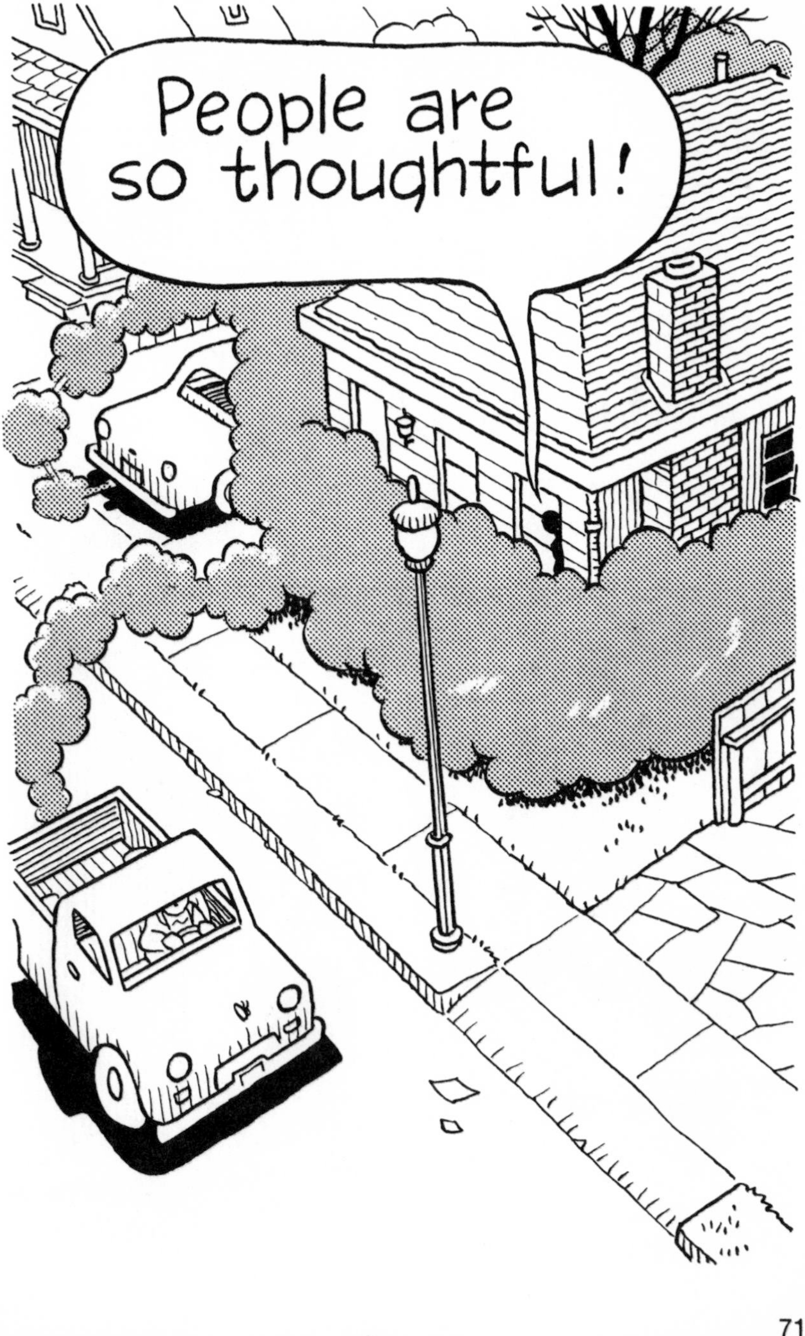
People are so thoughtful!

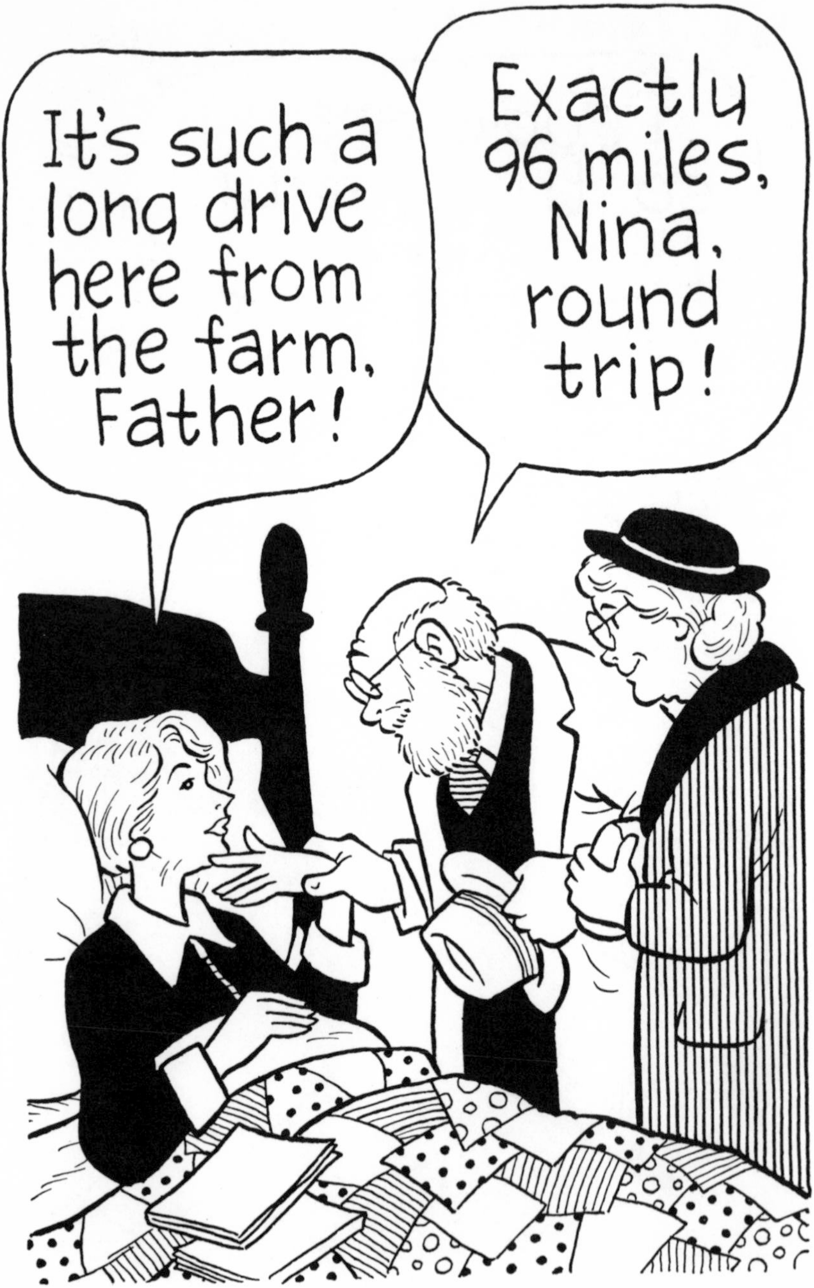
It's such a long drive here from the farm, Father!
Exactly 96 miles, Nina, round trip!

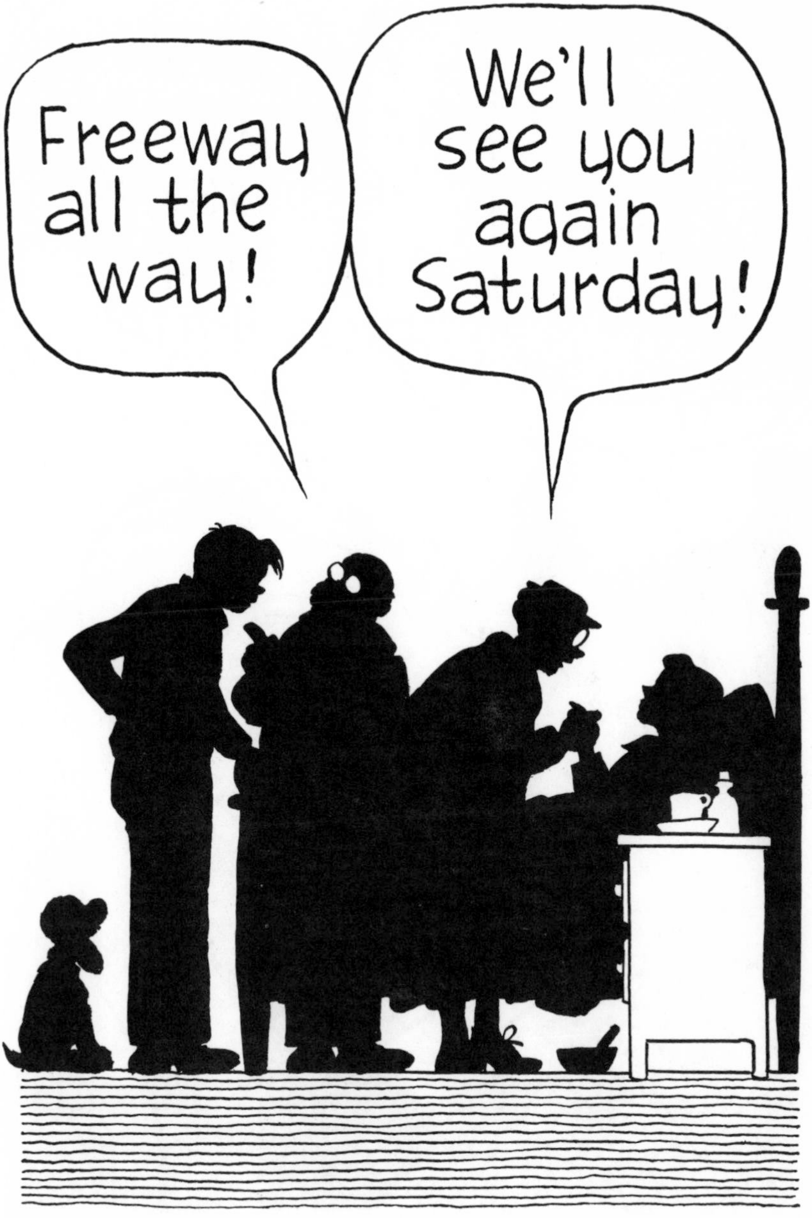
Freeway all the way!
We'll see you again Saturday!

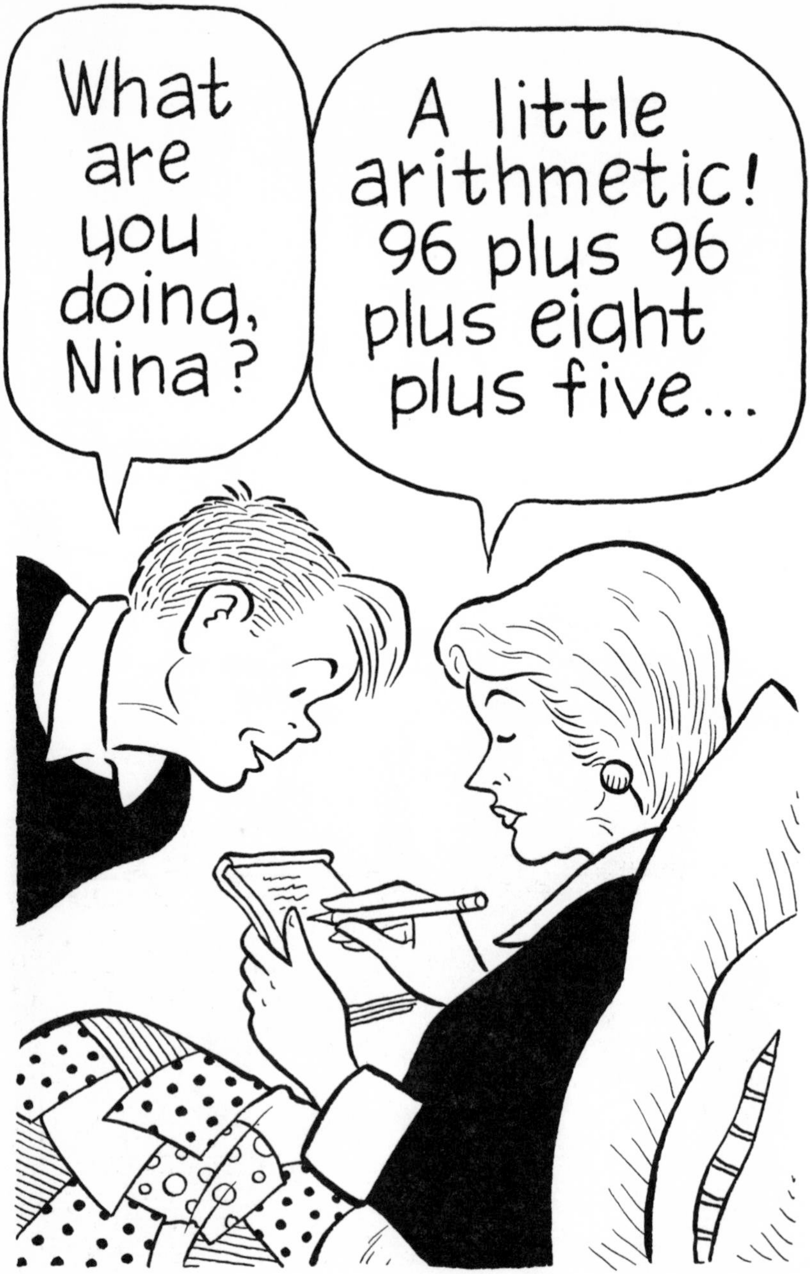
What are you doing, Nina?
A little arithmetic! 96 plus 96 plus eight plus five...

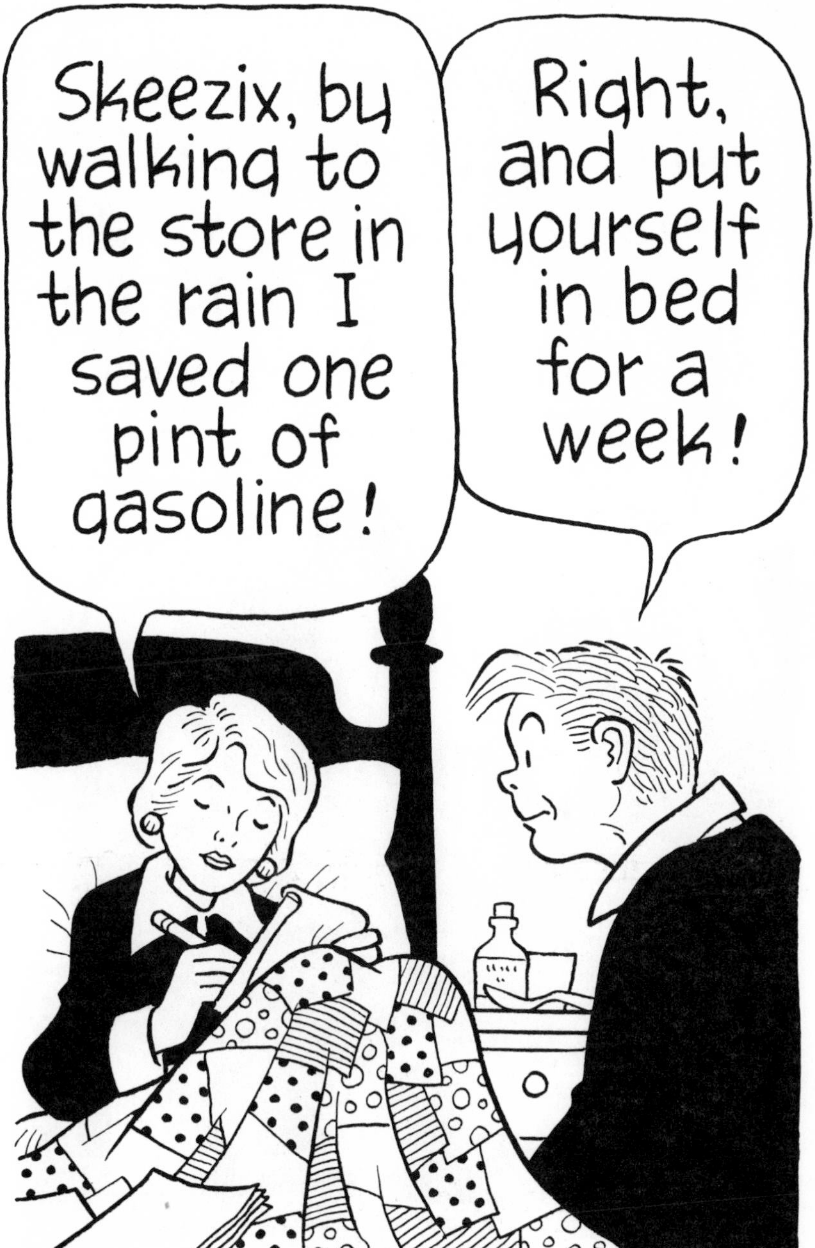
Skeezix, by walking to the store in the rain I saved one pint of gasoline!
Right, and put yourself in bed for a week!

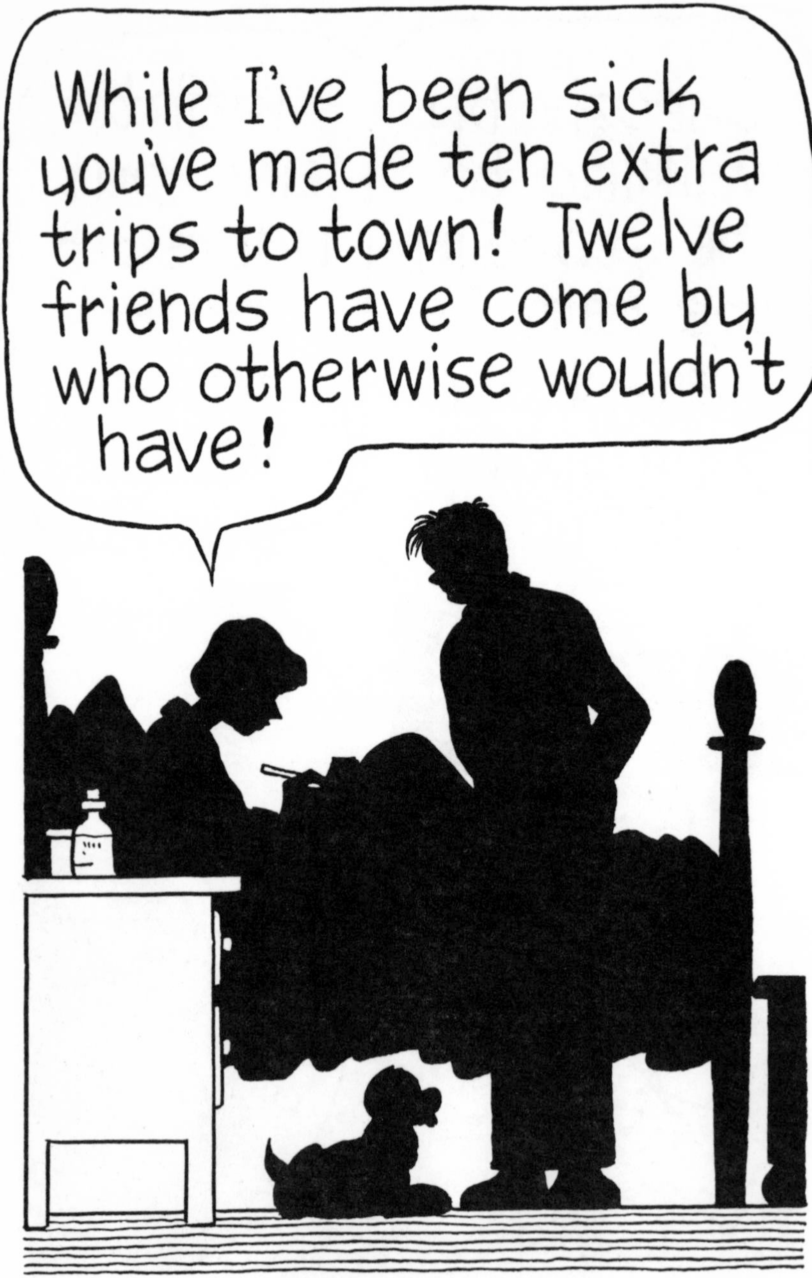
While I've been sick you've made ten extra trips to town! Twelve friends have come by who otherwise wouldn't have!

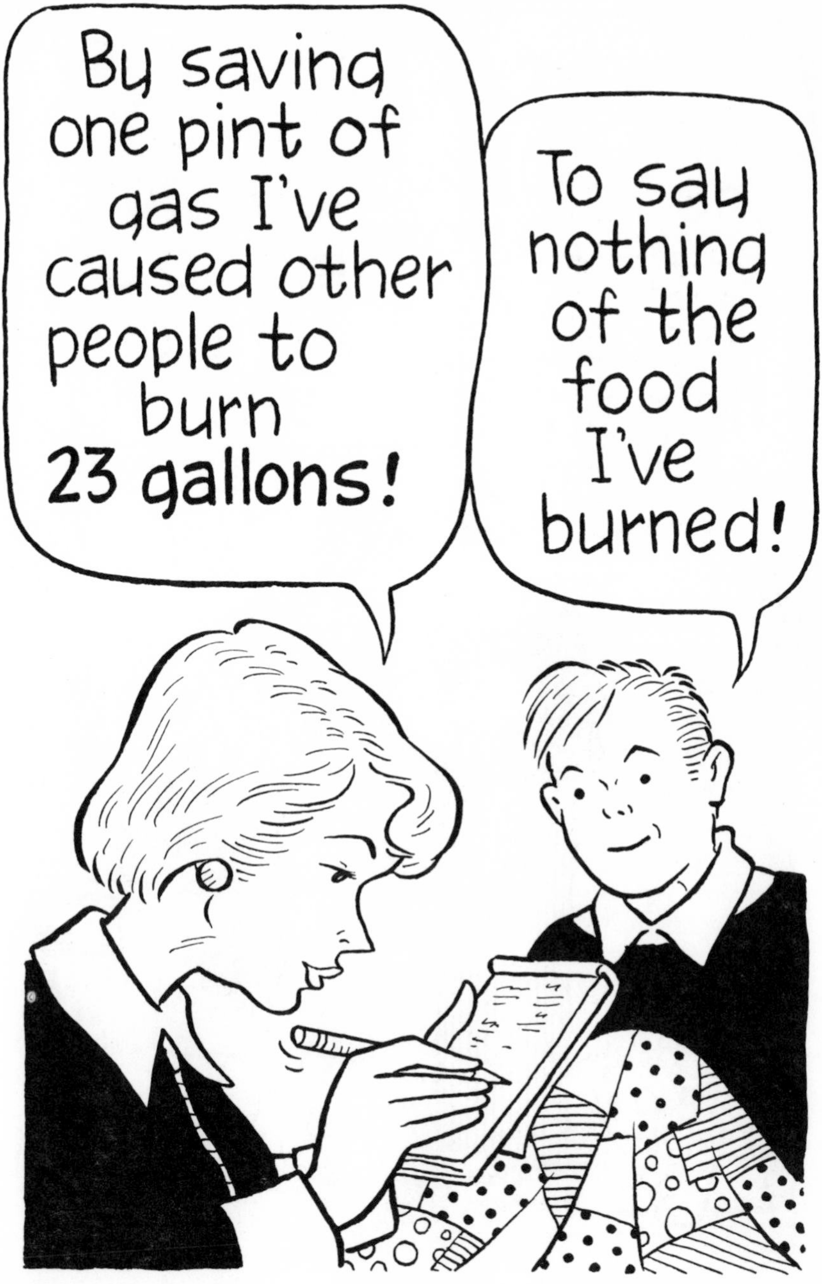
By saving one pint of gas I've caused other people to burn 23 gallons!
To say nothing of the food I've burned!

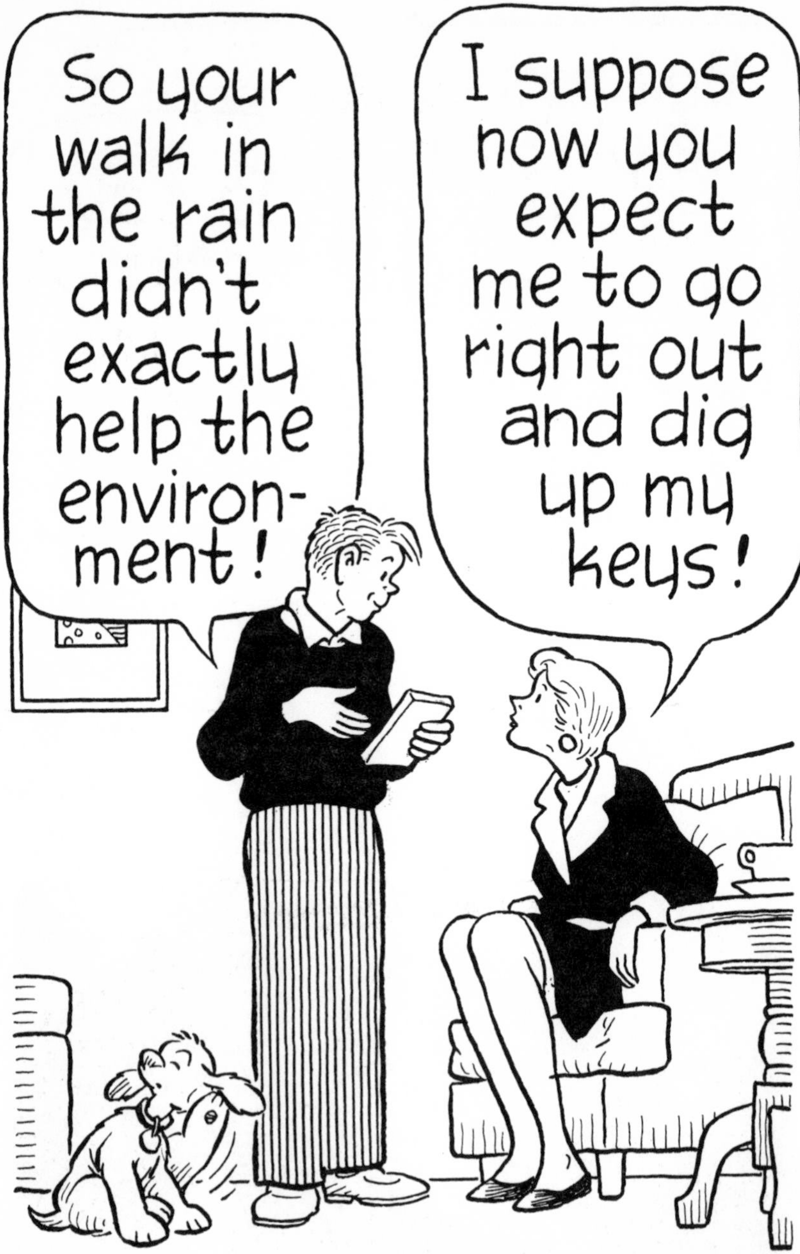
So your walk in the rain didn't exactly help the environment!
I suppose now you expect me to go right out and dig up my keys!

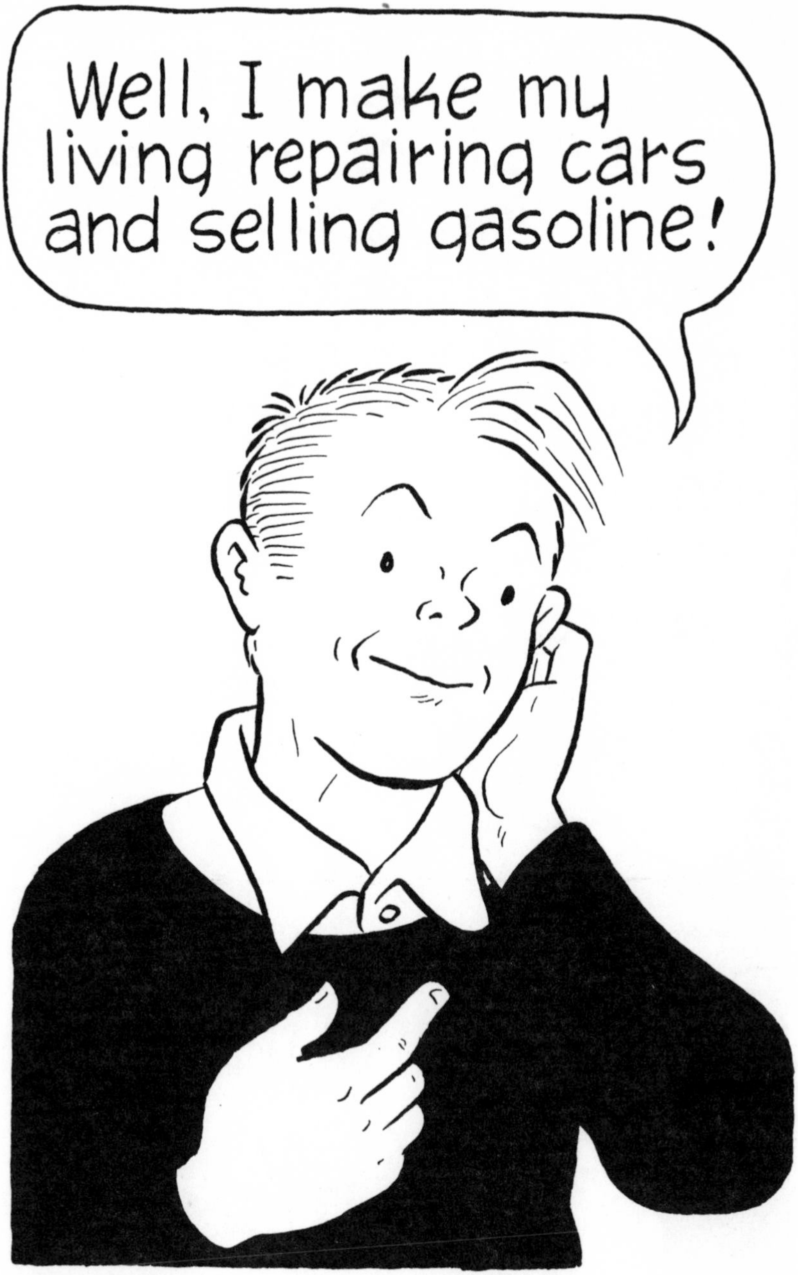
Well, I make my living repairing cars and selling gasoline!

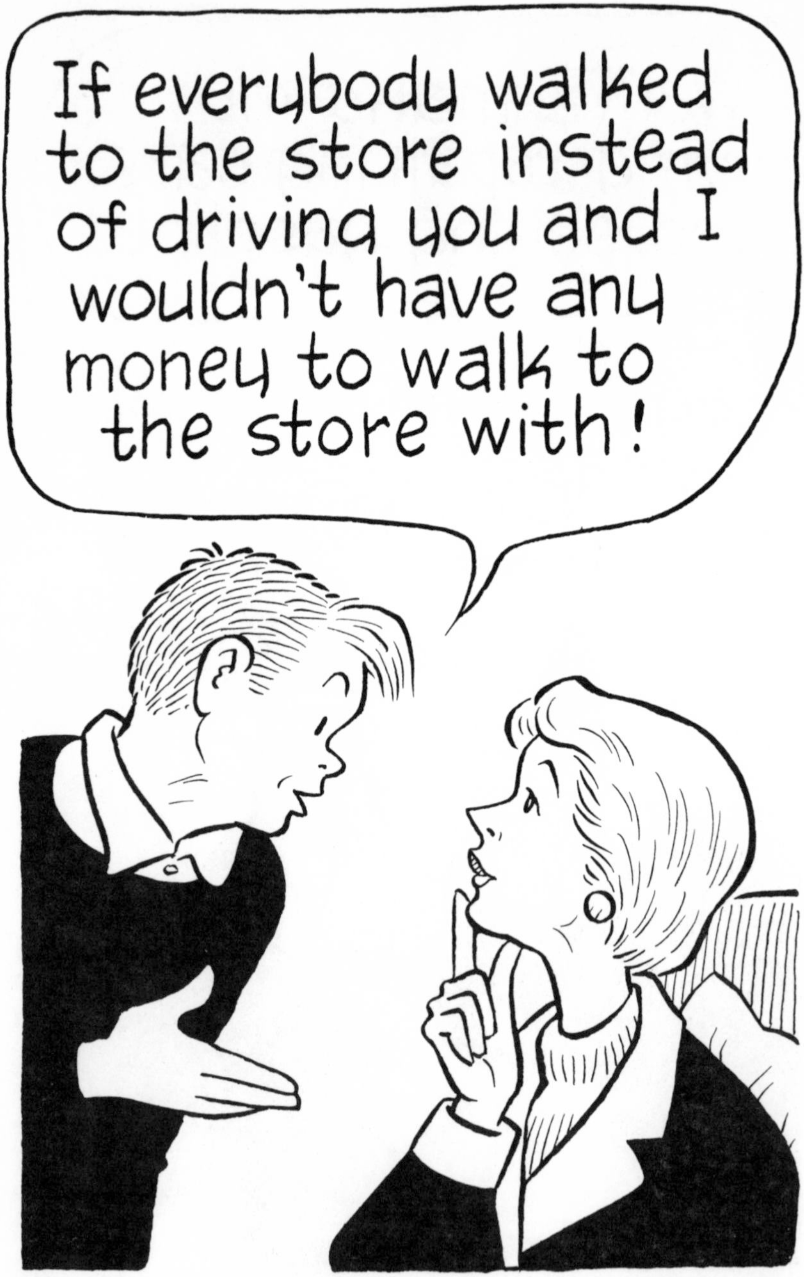
If everybody walked to the store instead of driving you and I wouldn't have any money to walk to the store with!

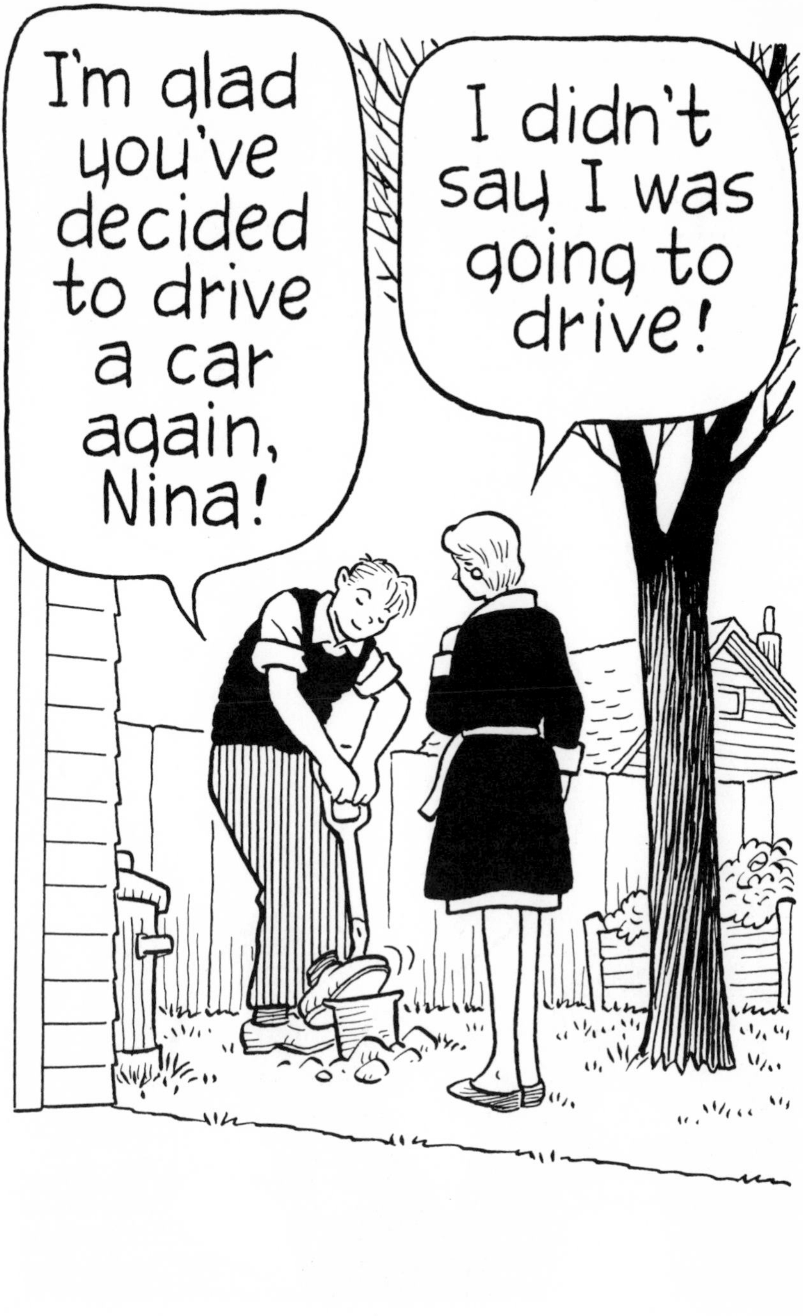
I'm glad you've decided to drive a car again, Nina!
I didn't say I was going to drive!

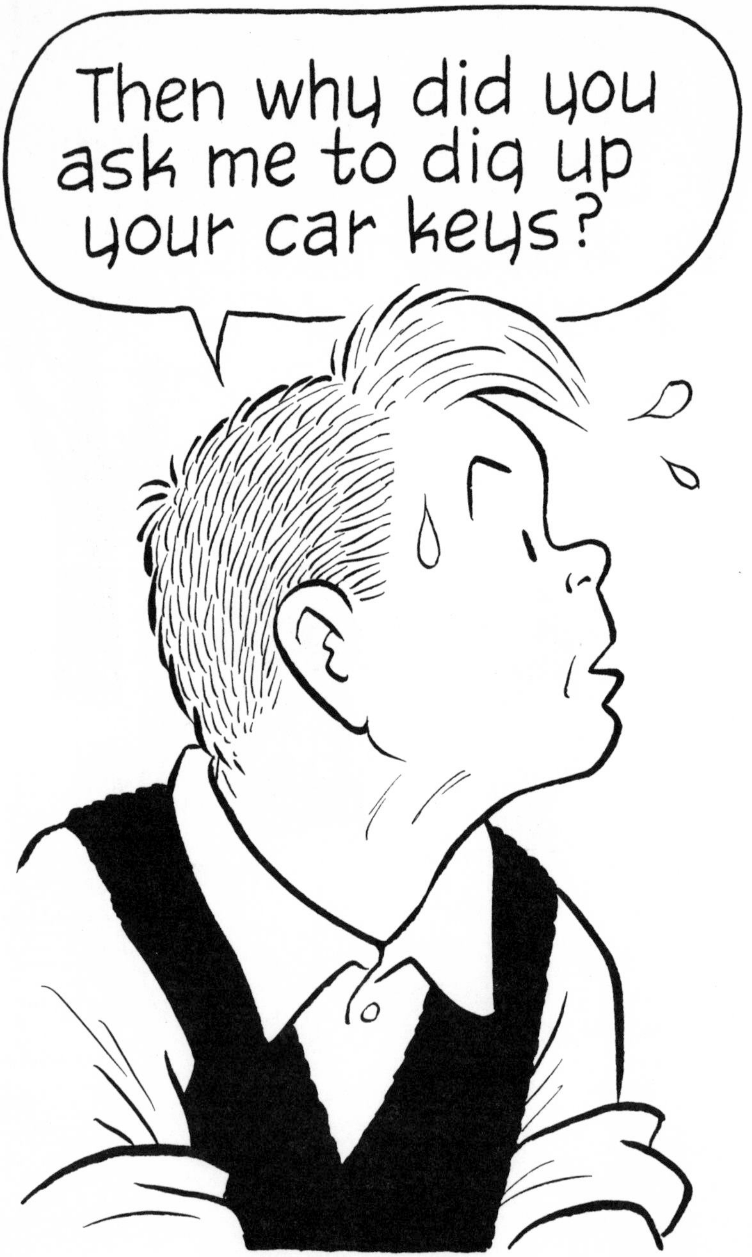
Then why did you ask me to dig up your car keys?

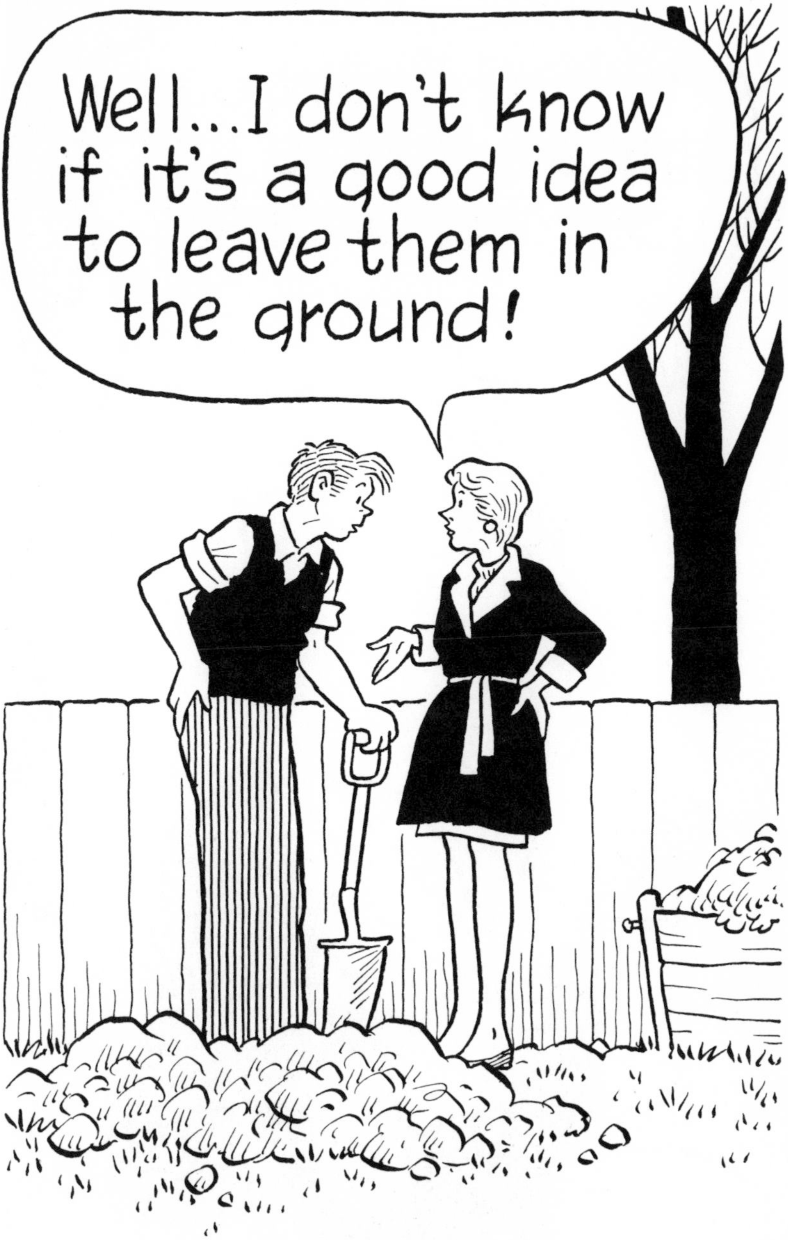
Well...I don't know if it's a good idea to leave them in the ground!

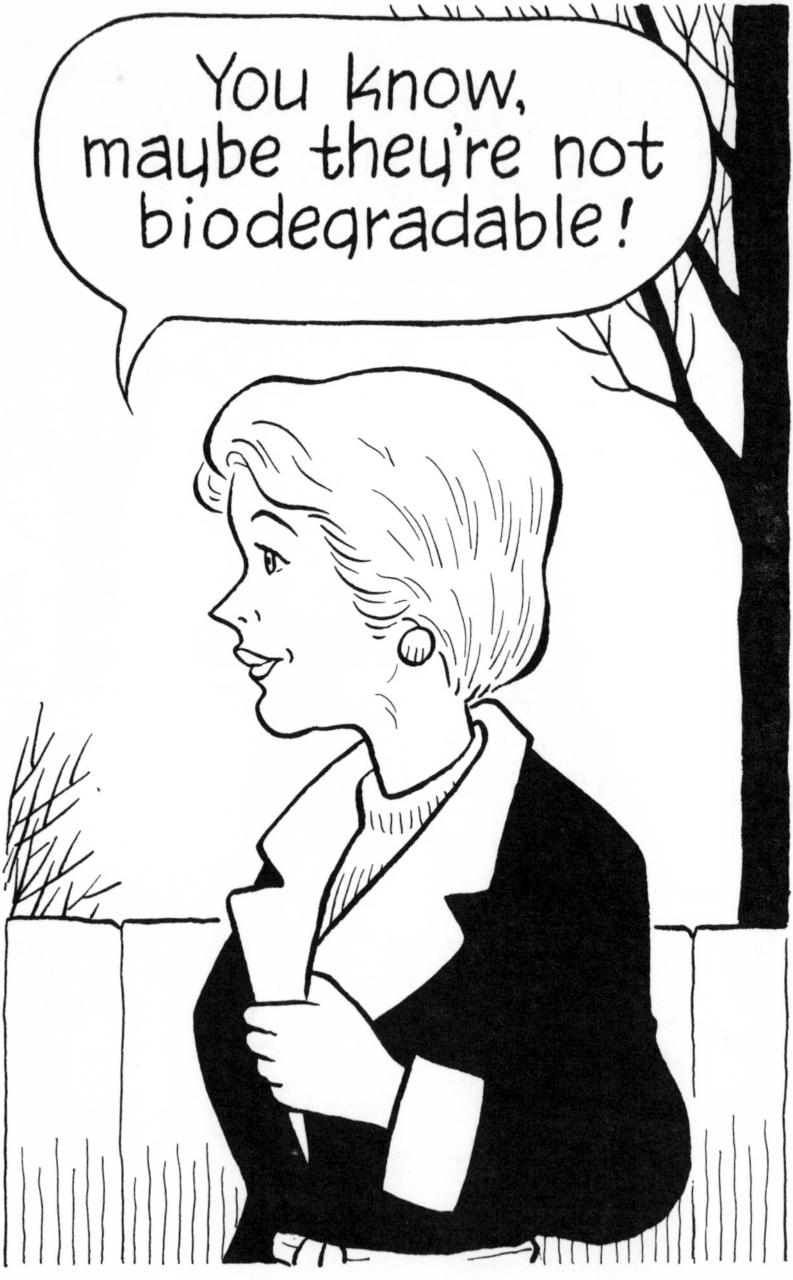
You know, maybe they're not biodegradable!

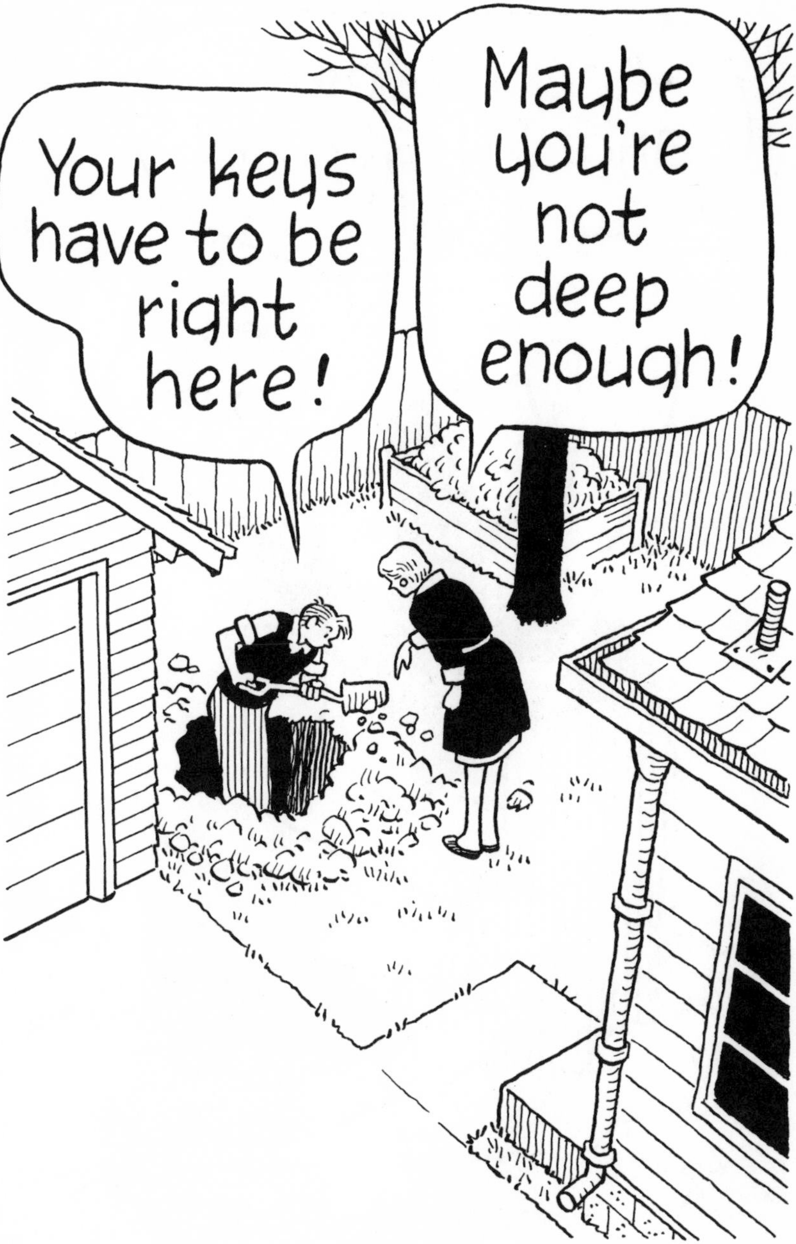
Your keys have to be right here!
Maybe you're not deep enough!

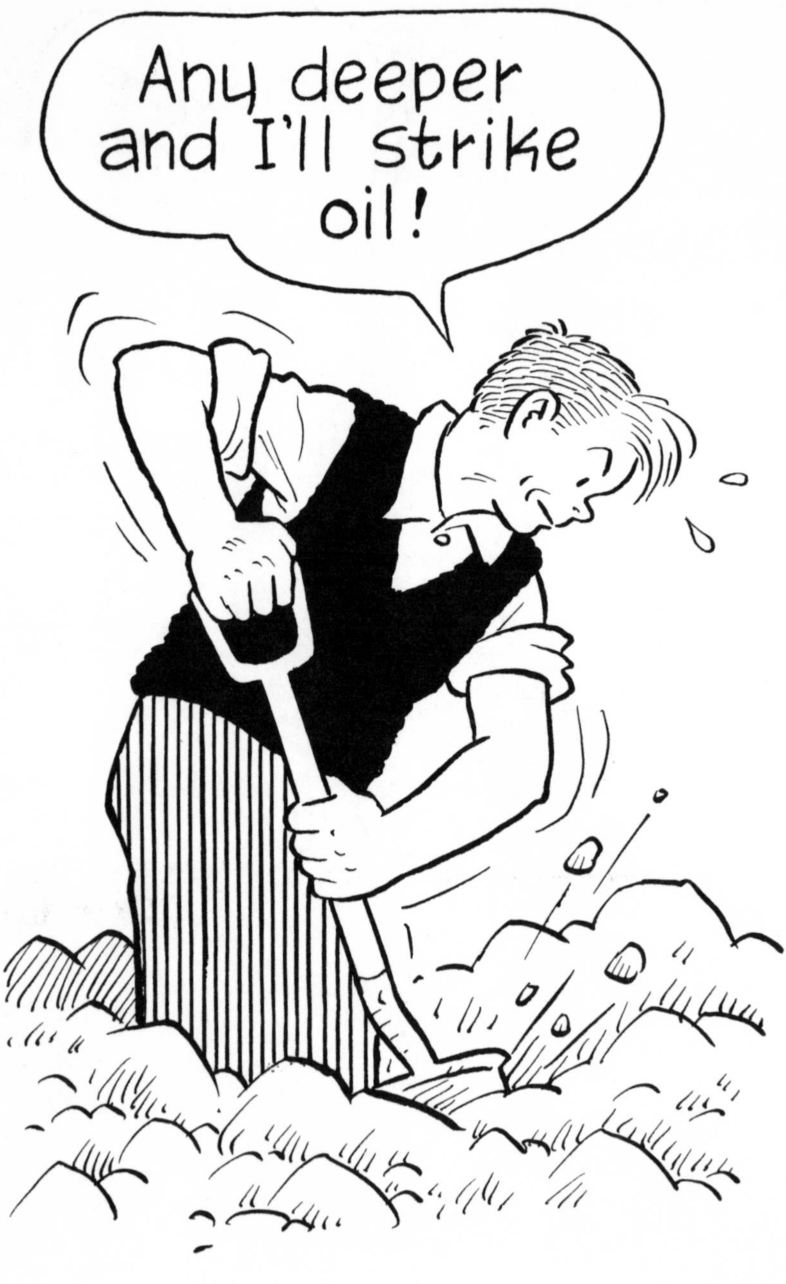
Any deeper and I'll strike oil!

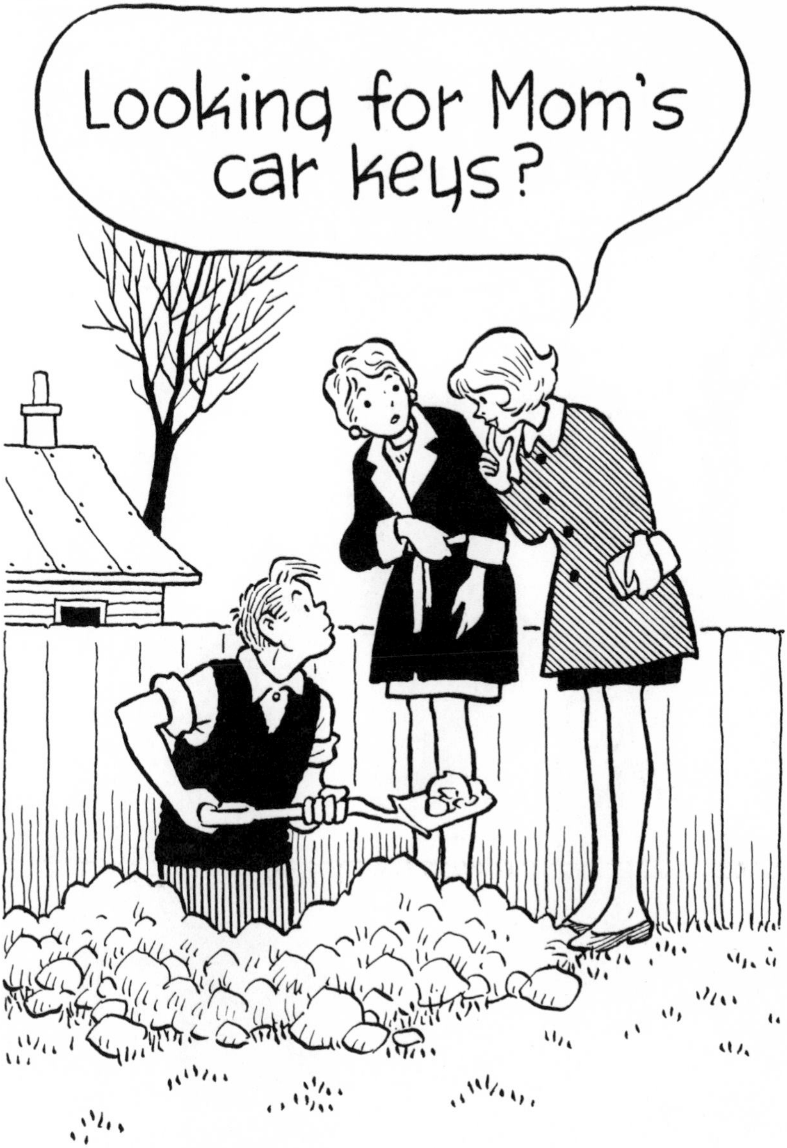
Looking for Mom's car keys?

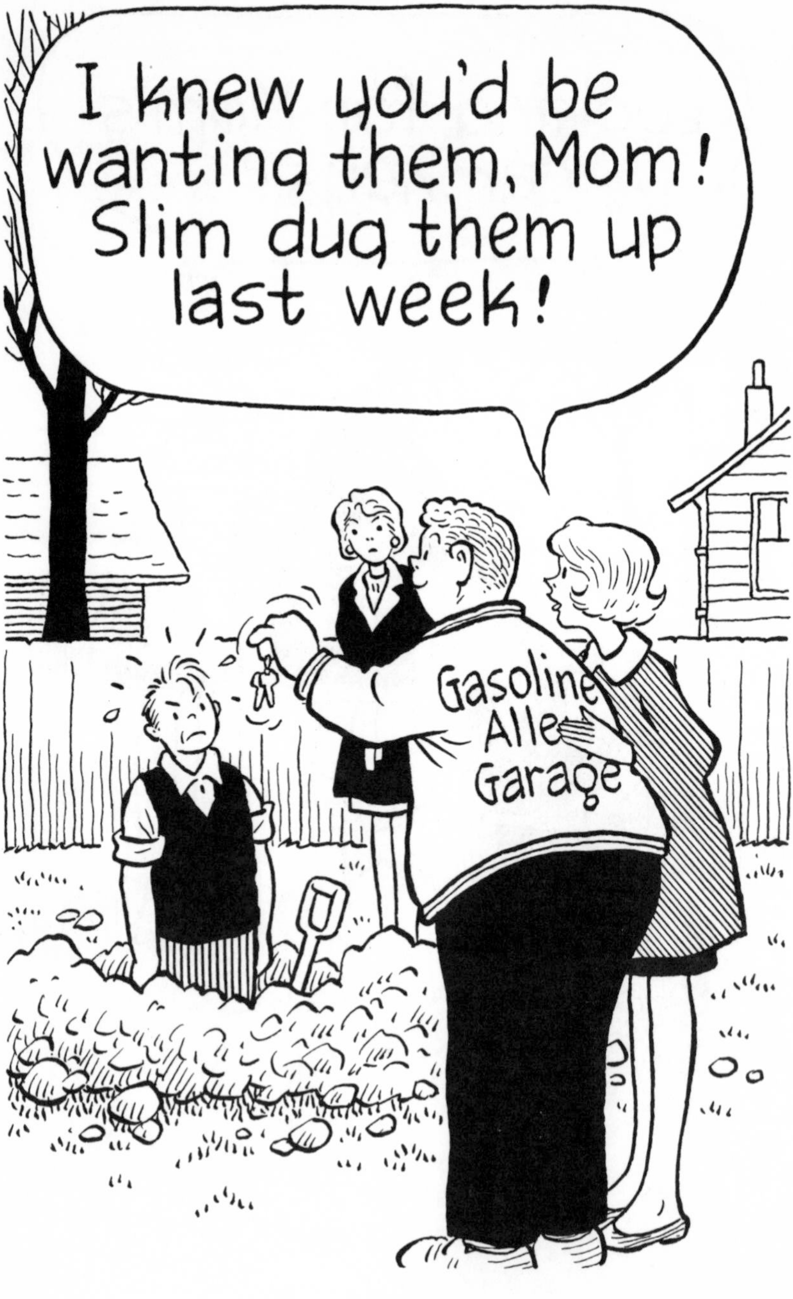
I knew you'd be wanting them, Mom! Slim dug them up last week!
Gasoline Alle Garage

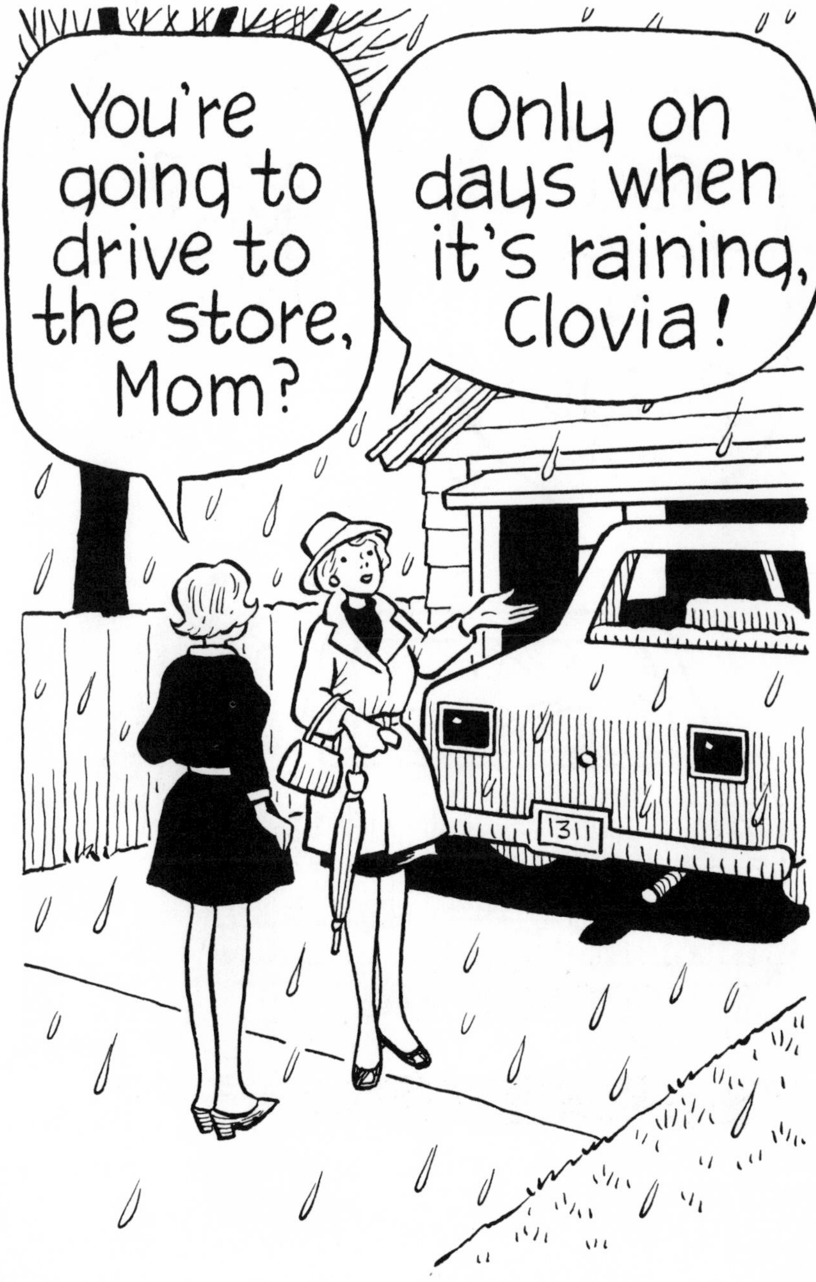
You're going to drive to the store, Mom?
Only on days when it's raining, Clovia!
1311

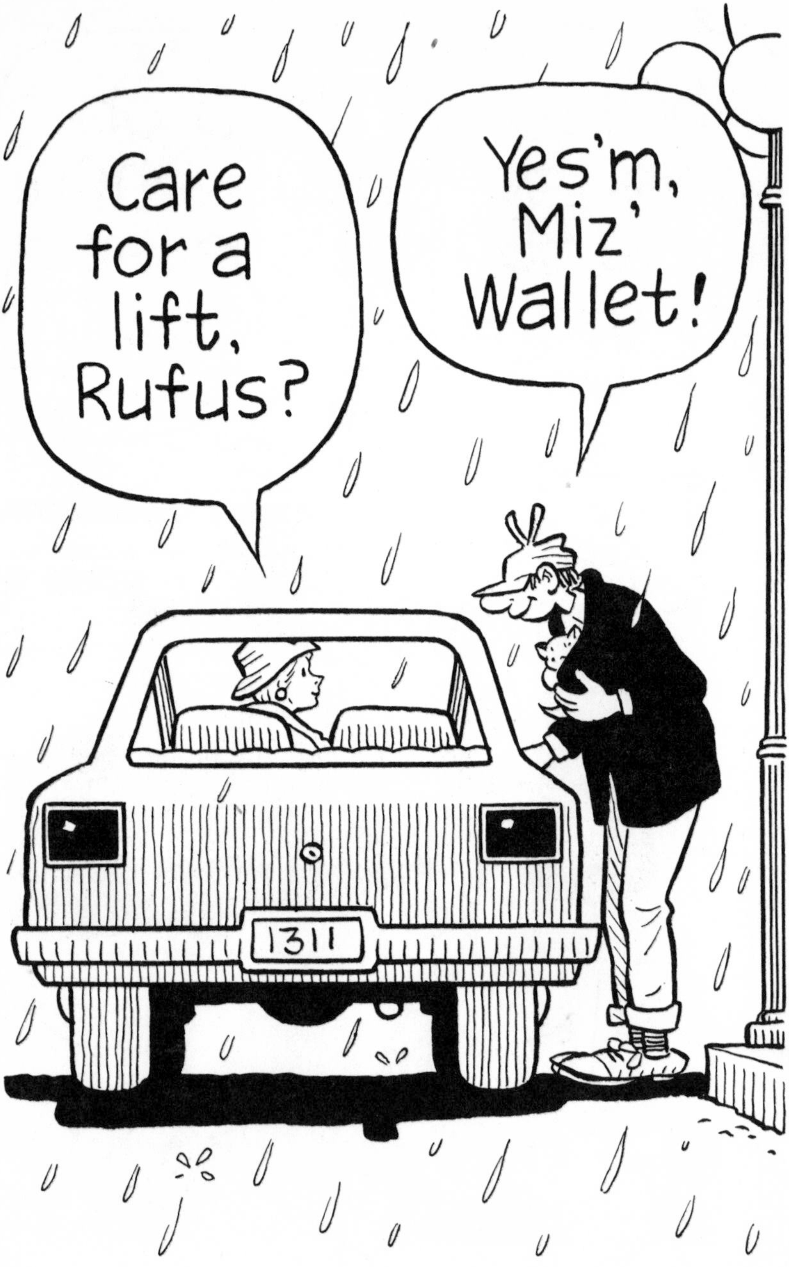
Care for a lift, Rufus?
Yes'm, Miz' Wallet!
1311

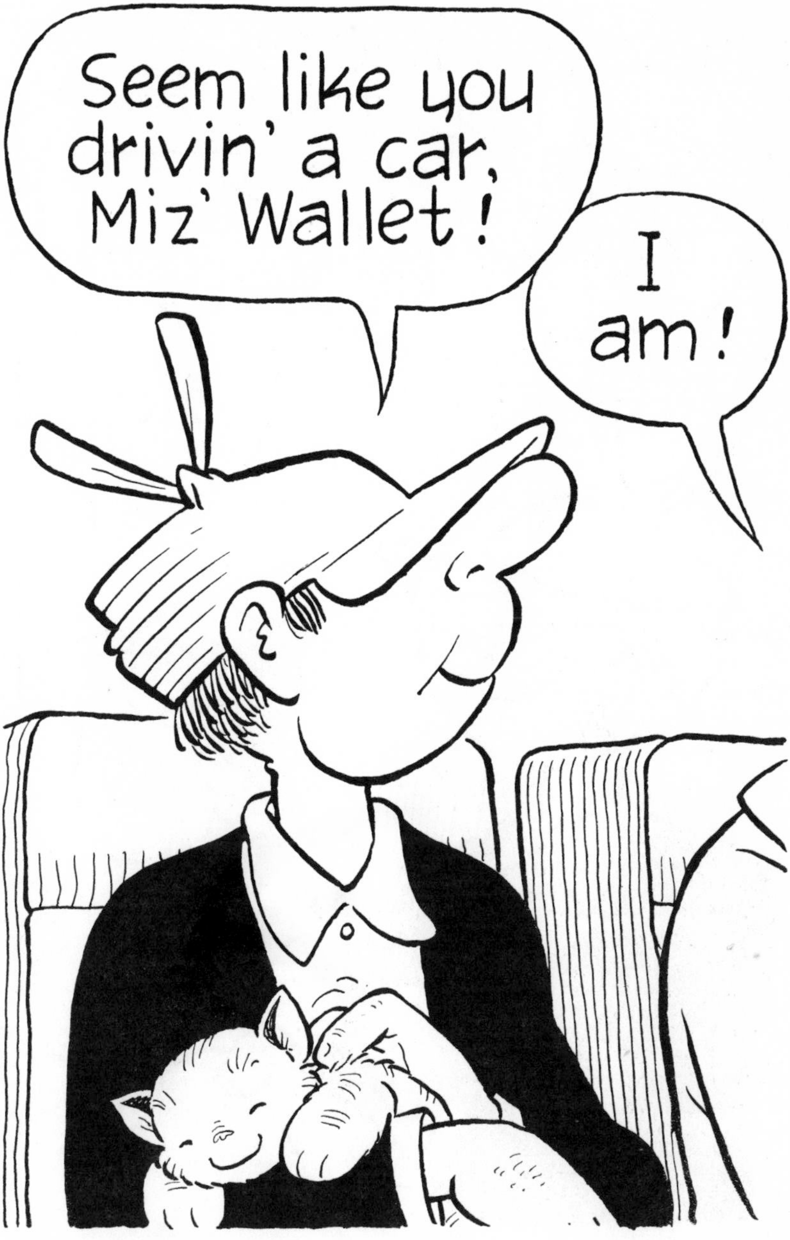
Seem like you drivin' a car, Miz' Wallet!
I am!

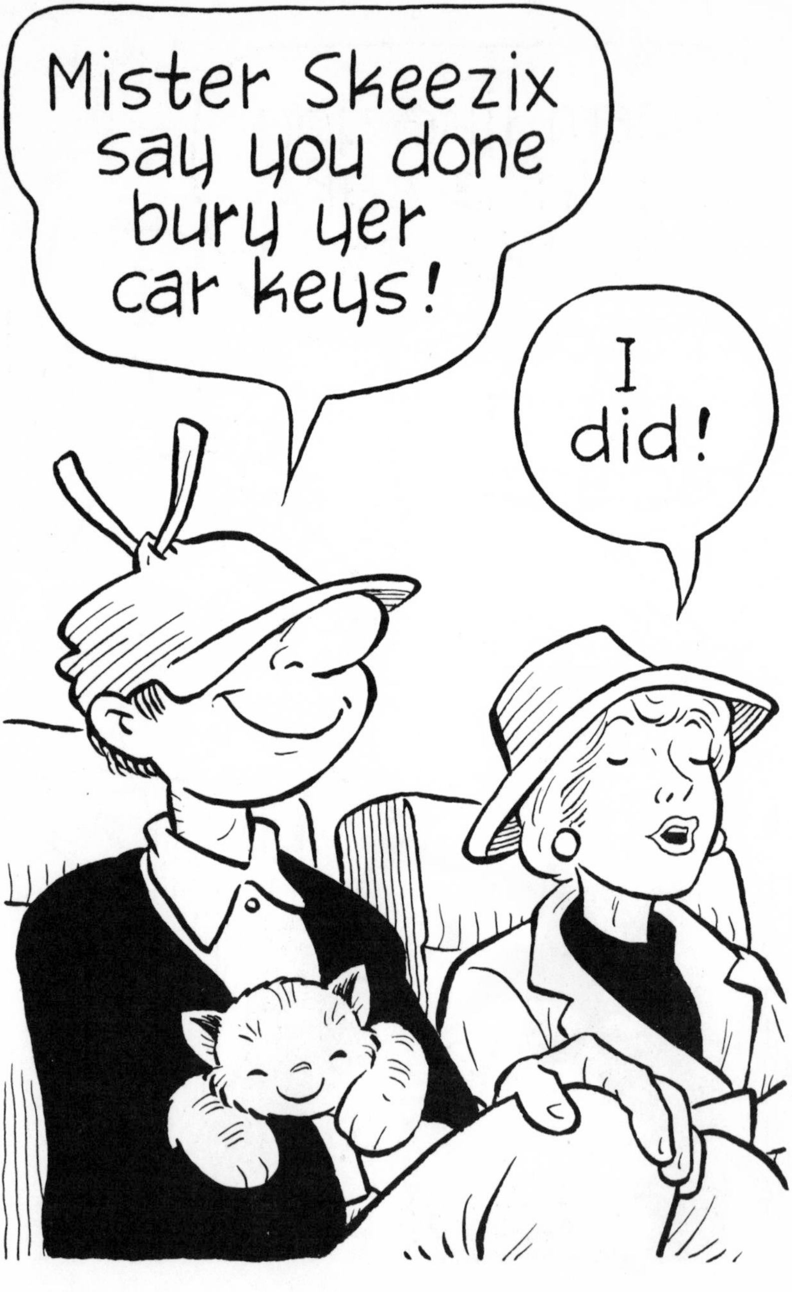
Mister Skeezix say you done bury yer car keys!
I did!

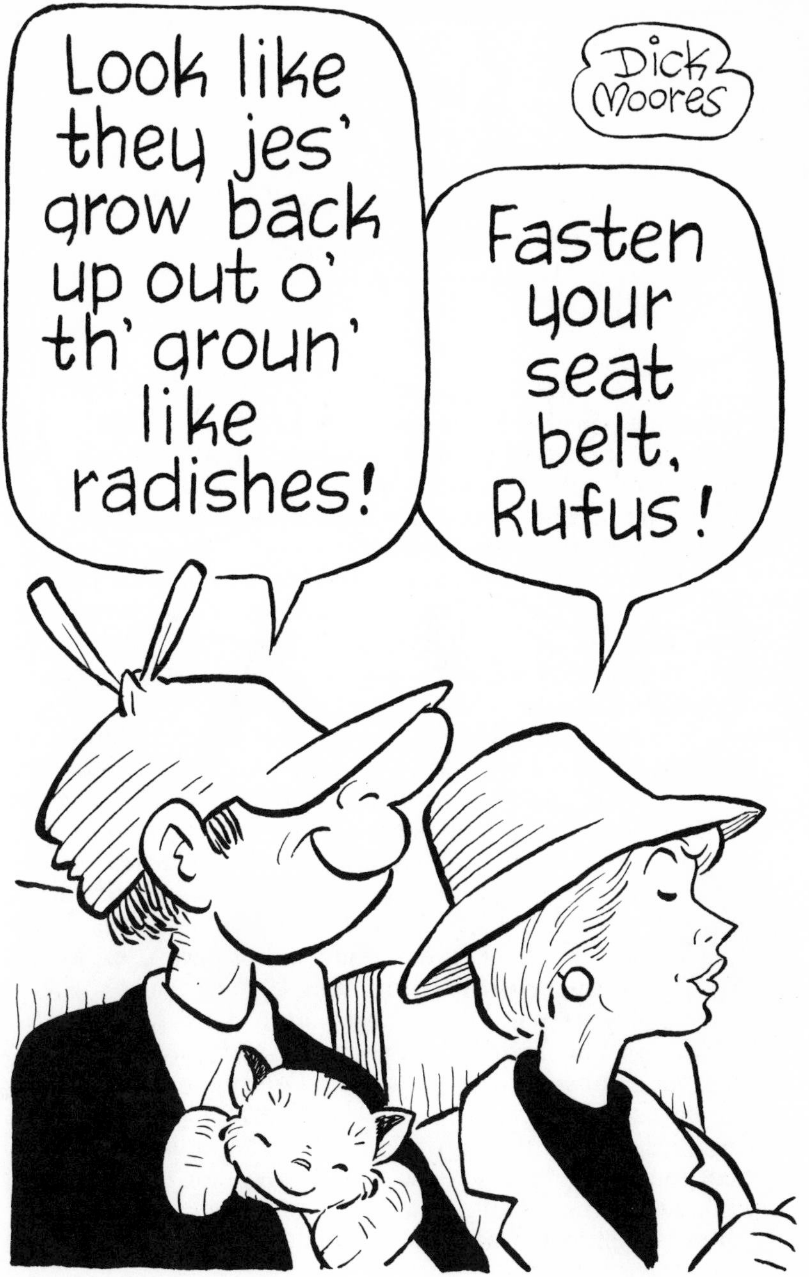
Dick Moores
Look like they jes' grow back up out o' th' groun' like radishes!
Fasten your seat belt, Rufus!

Afterword for Parents and Teachers

by Ralph Nader

A few years ago in an airport taxi, I heard a little girl, probably about nine years old, point to a factory and say to her mother, "Look at all that pollution!" A thought quickly crossed my mind: Wouldn't a nine-year-old child a decade earlier have said, "Look at all that smoke?"

There has been a remarkable change of perception among the young and among many grown-ups too. But, by far, not enough. Pollution is still too often thought of as dirty and annoying rather than as producing disease and damaging property.

Notice that Nina did not relate the pollution to human disease; neither did Joel or Skeezix. It was "smoke." It was "annoying." The air was going "to pot." Skeezix saw the situation as hopeless, for without the automobile the economy would collapse.

Nina made an effort to walk instead of drive. In real life there are more realistic alternatives. People can walk, share a car, take a bus, train, or a taxi, or form a car pool for commuting.

But personal choices are often not available because of our nation's imbalanced and auto-dominated surface transportation system. Personal choice, then, is not only restricted but also determined by what is most immediately profitable to the most powerful corporations. So there are highways for cars but no bikeways for bikes — with a few recent exceptions. Buses supplant trains and polluting engines win out over clean engines.

The sufferers and users of the automobile do not have the opportunity to decide matters of great public import with the makers of these products — the auto company officials. There are thousands of communities such as the one where Skeezix and Nina live. How many meetings occur between auto makers and auto users? Hardly any. Thus, people who care about their lungs, their health, and their community must go beyond Nina's very personal determination. They must organize as citizens in order that they themselves can shape the transportation system that their taxes and consumer dollars pay for. Many new technologies, new ways to get around on the ground efficiently and quickly and safely, exist. But, it will take citizen power to get the best ones adopted for their communities.

Because pollution does silent violence to health and because its tolls are not immediately visible but are exacted after a number of years have passed, people do not react against pollution as they would against a fire. "If it doesn't pinch, it doesn't hurt" is an easy attitude to adopt, *until* one stops to think. These chemicals, gases, and particulate matter that we call pollution rarely pinch people; oftentimes they are invisible, cannot be tasted, smelled, or touched. And people can psychologically adapt to these conditions with little grumbling. However, their lungs cannot adapt.

Restoration of the air, land, and water to the level of historic tolerance for humankind will depend on connecting what is happening to the lungs to what should happen in the mind. For, once abused, nature turns on its abusers. The forest and jungle animals, who refuse to soil their own nests, have known this for centuries. The lessons to be learned are clear.